Over the Next Hill & Still Rolling

Bob Phillips

HARVEST HOUSE PUBLISHERS
Eugene, Oregon 97402

Cover by Terry Dugan Design, Minneapolis, Minnesota

OVER THE NEXT HILL & STILL ROLLING

Copyright © 2001 by Bob Phillips
Published by Harvest House Publishers
Eugene, Oregon 97402

ISBN 0-7369-0619-3

Printed in the United States of America

03   04   05   06   /BC-CF/   9   8   7   6   5

Contents

1

You Know You're Over the Hill When...

You know you're over the hill when... people don't do double takes when you put on your flowered cap.

*

You know you're over the hill when...you own a pill counter.

*

You know you're over the hill when...the last candle on your birthday cake is lit. And the first one is almost completely melted.

*

You know you're over the hill when...you want to smack people who call you "sir."

*

You know you're over the hill when...you get short of breath opening the telephone directory.

✳

You know you're over the hill when…you have no guilt about appearing in pajamas and flicking the lights on and off when it's time for dinner guests to leave.

✳

You know you're over the hill when…you visit the information booth to find out where you parked your car.

✳

You know you're over the hill when…you install grab bars in your bathroom.

✳

You know you're over the hill when…you start waving to strangers from your porch, and get hostile if they don't wave back.

✳

You know you're over the hill when…visiting your aunt at the nursing home you're mistaken for one of the residents.

✳

You know you're over the hill when…you can easily name the last ten U.S. presidents.

✳

You know you're over the hill when…you amuse yourself with spur-of-the-moment sports, like Saturday afternoon walker races.

✳

You know you're over the hill when…you get into the car, sit down first, and then swing both legs in.

✳

You know you're over the hill when…you drop off your dry cleaning at the post office.

✳

You know you're over the hill when…you own only white underwear.

✳

You know you're over the hill when…a bad-hair day pertains to those growing out of your nose or ears.

✳

You know you're over the hill when…people are starting to give you gifts like stationery, dusting powder, and bath oil beads.

*

You know you're over the hill when...your spouse still snores, but now you can't hear it.

*

You know you're over the hill when...it doesn't take so long for summer to come again.

*

You know you're over the hill when...you're considering a move to a gated community and buying a Ford Crown Victoria.

*

You know you're over the hill when...kicking up your heels means lifting your feet so your wife can vacuum.

*

You know you're over the hill when...someone buys you padded hangers and drawer sachets.

*

You know you're over the hill when...your ears are hairier than your head.

*

You know you're over the hill when...you have a wart older than the paperboy.

*

You know you're over the hill when...happy hour is a nap.

*

You know you're over the hill when...you put tenderizer on puffed rice.

*

You know you're over the hill when...you would like to have a garage sale, but you're too embarrassed to have your neighbors see the odd assortment of junk you've collected over the years.

*

You know you're over the hill when...you always wipe your feet before you go inside.

*

You know you're over the hill when...you can't believe that the people in denture adhesive commercials are so young.

*

You know you're over the hill when...you refer to the refrigerator as the "icebox."

*

You know you're over the hill when...you just can't understand people who are intolerant.

*

You know you're over the hill when... friends start talking louder to you.

*

You know you're over the hill when...your favorite exercise is a good, brisk sit.

*

You know you're over the hill when...most of your dreams are reruns.

*

You know you're over the hill when...you know what *systolic* and *diastolic* mean.

*

You know you're over the hill when...the good side of the bed is the side closest to the bathroom.

✳

You know you're over the hill when...you blank out trying to remember why you are standing in front of a refrigerator with the door open.

✳

You know you're over the hill when... you're up to 2.75 on your reading glasses. But at restaurants, vanity prevents you from using them to study the menu.

✳

You know you're over the hill when...you actually start to obey the "Don't Walk" signal.

✳

You know you're over the hill when... blowing up balloons gets you winded.

✳

You know you're over the hill when...your children begin to look middle-aged.

✳

You know you're over the hill when... there's so much junk stored under your bed, there's no room for "dust bunnies."

*

You know you're over the hill when...lately you've been wondering how you would look driving a Winnebago.

2

A Laugh a Day Keeps the Wrinkles Away

You can't help getting older, but you don't have to get old.

George Burns

*

I'll miss being recognized and being fawned over. Now the only unrequited love I'll have is from my beagle.

Dan Glickman

*

I don't deserve this award, but I have arthritis and I don't deserve that either.

Jack Benny

*

Lying about your age is easier now that you sometimes forget what it is.

*

The years that a woman subtracts from her age are not lost. They are added to the ages of other women.

Diane De Poitiers

*

Don't worry about senility—when it hits you, you won't know it.

Bill Cosby

*

I'm 65, but if there were 15 months in every year, I'd only be 48.

James Thurber

*

She's not pushing 40, she's dragging it.

*

When I think of my dad as a little boy, I tend to think of him in black and white.

*

You can't take it with you. You never see a U-Haul following a hearse.

Arnold Glasow

*

Pushing 40? She's clinging onto it for dear life.

*

That's the problem with old age—there's not much future in it.

*

She was so old when she went to school they didn't have history.

Rodney Dangerfield

*

Age is nothing more than mind over matter. If you don't mind, it doesn't matter.

Satchel Paige

*

If you don't go to people's funerals, they won't come to yours.

*

A woman may grow old before her time trying to look young after her time.

Herbert V. Prochnow

*

The secret to longevity is to keep breathing.

Sophie Tucker

*

Life is like a taxi ride—the meter keeps on ticking whether you're getting anywhere or not.

*

I advise you to go on living solely to enrage those who are paying your annuities. It is the only pleasure I have left.

Voltaire

*

A youthful figure is what you get when you ask a woman her age.

*

I am just turning 40 and taking my time about it.

Harold Lloyd

*

To the nation's best-kept secret—your true age.

*

At 16 I was stupid, confused, insecure, and indecisive. At 25 I was wise, self-confident, pre-possessing, and assertive. At 45 I am stupid, confused, insecure, and indecisive. Who would have supposed that maturity is only a short break in adolescence?

Jules Feiffer

*

She claims that she's still 39 years old. I can't understand it...when I was 39, it only lasted a year!

*

The only time in our lives we like to get old is when we're kids. If you're less than 10 years old you're so excited about aging that you think in fractions. How old are you? Six and a half! You're never 36 and a half.

*

When it comes to staying young, a mind-lift beats a face-lift any day.

Marty Bucella

*

All I have to live on now is macaroni and memorial services.

Margot Asquith

*

I've been told that 50 is the age when *happy* and *birthday* seem to go their separate ways.

*

You know you're middle-aged when you start making the distinction between "young old" people and "old old" people.

*

Old age does have some advantages. Not only can you sing while you shower, you can sing while you brush your teeth.

George Jessel

*

In her later years the famous actress Sarah Bernhardt lived in an apartment high over Paris. An old admirer climbed all the stairs to see her one day. He asked her breathlessly, "Why do you live so high up?" "Dear friend," she replied, "it is the only way I can still make the hearts of men beat faster."

*

As an aged man lay dying in the hospital, he summoned his nurse. "Would you call to me my lawyer and my doctor, right away?" he requested.

Within a half hour both the man's doctor and his attorney were at his side. The man's breathing was labored by this time, but he remained silent.

The attorney spoke. "What did you need us for?"

The reply came momentarily. "Nothing," he said. "I have heard Jesus died between two thieves," he continued. "I wanted to know what it felt like."

*

Police were called to help restore order at the Presbyterian Home for the Aged, the scene of a weeklong revolt. Three militant octogenarians were arrested after a scuffle in the north parlor. These three who were arrested were identified as leaders of the activist group that seized control of the parlor three days earlier and locked the matron in the closet.

One reason given for the protest: "We have a bunch of young whippersnappers running things around here, and we don't trust anybody under 65." Another reason from a different activist: "What is the sense of living a long time if some 50-year-old kid is going to tell you what to do?"

3

Name the Year Quiz— The 1930s

1. What Year Was It? _____

The first issue of *Life* magazine

Dale Carnegie writes *How to Win Friends and Influence People*

Cole Porter writes "Easy to Love"

Bruno Hauptman is convicted of killing the Lindbergh baby

*

2. What Year Was It? _____

Fritos corn chips are introduced

Amelia Earhart becomes the first woman to fly the Atlantic solo

The movie: *A Farewell to Arms*

Jonny Weismuller debuts in the *Tarzan* movies

Shirley Temple makes her first movie

＊

3.　What Year Was It? _____

Hoagy Carmichael writes "Georgia on My Mind"

The movie: *All Quiet on the Western Front*

Contract bridge becomes a popular card game

The Blondie comic strip debuts

＊

4.　What Year Was It? _____

Nylon stockings are first sold

The movie: *Gone with the Wind*

The movie: *The Wizard of Oz*

The average wage was 62 cents per hour

The radio programs: *The Shadow* and *Captain Midnight*

The first televised baseball game

*

5.   What Year Was It? _____

Irving Berlin writes "Easter Parade"

Spam is invented and begins a new era of processed foods

The movie: *King Kong*

The movie: *Little Women,* starring Katherine Hepburn

*

6.   What Year Was It? _____

The 40-hour workweek is introduced

The radio program: "War of the Worlds," broadcast by Orson Wells

The song: "Jeepers, Creepers"

Porsche designs the Volkswagen Beetle

*

7.   What Year Was It? _____

"The Star-Spangled Banner" is made the official national anthem

The song: "When the Moon Comes over the Mountain"

Al Capone jailed for income-tax evasion

The movie: *Front Page*

*

8. What Year Was It? _____

The game Monopoly is introduced

Saddle shoes with ankle socks and pillbox hats become the fad…along with the jitterbug, platform shoes, and sunglasses

The rumba becomes the fashionable dance

Alcoholics Anonymous is organized

*

9. What Year Was It? _____

The song: "All I Do Is Dream of You"

The first coin Laundromat

The movie: *The Thin Man*

Popular radio programs included *Flash Gordon, Buck Rogers,* and the *Lone Ranger*

*

10. What Year Was It? _____

The first feature-length cartoon: *Snow White*

The Golden Gate Bridge opens in San Francisco

Amelia Earhart is lost in the Pacific

The Hindenberg disaster

*

Answers
1. 1936 2. 1932 3. 1930 4. 1939 5. 1933 6. 1938 7. 1931 8. 1935 9. 1934 10. 1937

4

Wisdom of the Ages

The age of a woman doesn't mean a thing. The best tunes are played on the oldest fiddles.

Sigmund Z. Engel

*

No matter how old a mother is, she still watches her middle-aged children for signs of improvement.

Florida Scott-Maxwell

*

Growing old is no more than a bad habit which a busy man has not time to form.

Andre Maurois

*

I used to dread getting older because I thought I would not be able to do all the things I wanted to do, but now that I am older I find that I don't want to do them.

Lady Nancy Astor

*

A man is not old until regrets take the place of dreams.

John Barrymore

*

I have achieved my 70 years in the usual way: by sticking strictly to a scheme of life which would kill anybody else. It sounds like an exaggeration, but that is really the common rule for attaining old age.

*

As I give thought to the matter, I find four causes for the apparent misery of old age; first, it withdraws us from active accomplishments; second, it renders the body less powerful; third, it deprives us of almost all forms of enjoyment; fourth, it stands not far from death.

Marcus Tullius Cicero

*

A man over 90 is a great comfort to all his elderly neighbors: He is a picket guard at the extreme outpost; and the young folks of 60 and 70 feel that the enemy must get by him before he can come near their camp.

Oliver Wendell Holmes

*

I am getting old and the sign of old age is that I begin to philosophize and ponder over problems which should not be my concern at all.

Jawaharlal Nehru

*

There's one advantage to being 102. There's no peer pressure.

Dennis Wolfberg

*

I have always felt that a woman has a right to treat the subject of her age with ambiguity until, perhaps, she passes into the realm of over 90. Then it is better she be candid with herself and with the world.

Helena Rubinstein

*

Youth goes in a flock, manhood in pairs, and old age alone.

*

The whiter my hair becomes, the more ready people are to believe what I say.

*

Old boys have their playthings as well as young ones; the difference is only in the price.
Benjamin Franklin

*

We are but older children, dear, who fret to find our bedtime near.

Lewis Carroll

*

A person is always startled when he hears himself seriously called an old man for the first time.

Oliver Wendell Holmes

*

An old man in the house is a good sign.
Benjamin Franklin

*

Wrinkles are the crannies and footholds on the smooth visage of life to which man can cling and gain some comfort and security.

*

Nature is full of freaks, and now puts an old head on young shoulders, and then a young heart beating under fourscore winters.
Ralph Waldo Emerson

*

Old age is the most unexpected of all the things that happen to a man.

Leon Trotsky

*

I never think of the future. It comes soon enough.

Albert Einstein

*

The first half of our lives is ruined by our parents and the second half by our children.

Clarence Darrow

*

In old age one again becomes a child.

*

Age mellows some people; others it makes rotten.

*

Youth has a beautiful face and old age a beautiful soul.

*

Life is a continual process of getting used to things we never expected.

*

The tragedy of old age is not that one is old, but that one is young.

Oscar Wilde

*

Life is like playing a violin solo in public and learning the instrument as one goes on.

Samuel Butler

5

Tombstone Humor

On the tombstone of a careless cowboy:
Here lies a man whose crown was won
by blowing in an empty gun.

*

He wrote learnedly, preached painfully,
lived piously, died peacefully.

Bishop Jewel

*

Here lie the remains of poor Christopher Type
The rest of him couldn't be found:
He sat on a powder cask, smoking a pipe,
While the wind blew the ashes around.

*

This is what I expected but not so soon.

*

God works a wonder now and then,
He, though a lawyer, was an honest man.

*

Here lies the body of our Anna
Done to death by a banana
It wasn't the fruit that laid her low
But the skin of the thing that made her go.

*

Epitaph on a hypochondriac's grave: I
Told You I Was Sick.

*

I have had enough.

Golda Meir

*

Epitaph of an attorney, Rockford, Illinois:
The defense rests.

*

Here lies the body
Of Jonathan Blake
Stepped on the gas
Instead of the brake.

*

On the tombstone of an Auctioneer:
Going, Going, Gone.

*

Here lies the body of Mary Anne
Safe in the arms of Abraham.
All very well for Mary Anne
But how about poor Abraham?

*

Deep in this grave lies lazy Dai
Waiting the last great trump on high.
If he's as fond of his grave as he's fond of
his bed
He'll be the last man up when that roll
call's said.

*

I always wait for *The Times* each morning.
I look at the obituary column, and if I'm not
in it, I go to work.

A. E. Matthews

*

Here lies a poor woman who always was
tired,
For she lived in a place where help wasn't
hired,
Her last words on earth were, "Dear
friends, I am going,
Where washing ain't done nor cooking
nor sewing
And everything there is exact to my wishes,

For there they don't eat, there's no washing of dishes,

I'll be where loud anthems will always be ringing

(But having no voice, I'll be out of the singing).

Don't mourn for me now, don't grieve for me never,

For I'm going to do nothing for ever and ever."

*

Keep the line moving.

Jack Paar

*

Here lies Nunnally Johnson. If I don't come back, go right ahead without me.

Nunnally Johnson

*

Here lies John Bunn

Who was killed by a gun.

His name wasn't Bunn, but his real name was Wood,

But Wood wouldn't rhyme with gun,

So I thought Bunn should.

*

Here lies a man who was killed by lightning;
He died when his prospects seemed to be brightening.
He might have cut a flash in this world of trouble,
But the flash cut him, and he lies in the stubble.

*

Dorothy Parker
(1893-1967)
Excuse my Dust.

*

Here lie I, and no wonder I'm dead,
For the wheel of a wagon went over my head.

*

Here lies John Yeast. Pardon me for not rising.

*

Here lies the bones of Richard Lawton
Whose death alas! was strangely brought on.
Trying his corns one day to mow off.
His razor slipped and cut his toe off.
His toe or rather what it grew to,

An inflammation quickly grew too.
Which took alas! to mortifying
And was the cause of Richard's dying.

✻

Here lies the body of Bob Dent;
He kicked up his heels and to Hell he went.

✻

Samuel Foote, Comedian (1720–77)
Here lies one Foote,
Whose death may thousands save,
For death has now one foot within the grave.

✻

Eternal epitaph: "Pause, Stranger, when you pass me by. As you are now, so once was I. As I am now, so you will be. So prepare for death and follow me." An unknown passerby read those words and underneath scratched this reply: "To follow you I'm not content, until I know which way you went."

J. M. Kennedy

✻

Over my dead body!

George F. Kaufman

✻

This is on me.

*

Here lies an atheist
All dressed up
And no place to go.

*

Here lies Fred,
Who was alive and is dead;
Had it been his father,
I had much rather;
Had it been his brother,
Still better than another;
Had it been his sister,
No one would have missed her;
Had it been the whole generation,
Still better for the nation:
But since 'tis only Fred,
Who was alive and is dead,
There's no more to be said.

6

Famous Family Phrases of the Middle-Aged

You can only get a dog if you promise to take care of it.

*

How many times do I have to tell you?

*

I'm not going to start this car until you kids settle down and stop fighting.

*

How come you never call?

*

You don't use the bathroom this often at home.

*

Takes one to know one.

＊

No, we're not there yet.

＊

Why don't you go outside and play?

＊

I can't play with you now. I have work to do.

＊

Don't expect your problems to go away by themselves.

＊

If you can't do it right, don't bother doing it at all.

＊

Whatever you say, it's double.

＊

You can do anything you set your mind to.

＊

If you say that again, I'll wash your mouth out with soap.

*

Don't eat the chocolate bunny now; it'll spoil your dinner.

*

Who said life is supposed to be fair?

*

Don't cry over spilled milk. Let the cat lick it up.

*

You're grounded. You ain't goin' nowhere.

*

If I've told you once, I've told you a thousand times.

*

Finders keepers, losers weepers.

*

OK, tell me why you did it, but I don't want to hear any excuses.

*

You're only five. If you want to live to see six, you'll do what I say.

*

If you don't stop crying, I'll give you something to cry about.

*

If you fall out of that tree and break your leg, don't come running to me.

*

Do what I say, not what I do.

*

If you watch too much TV, your brains will turn to mush.

*

If all your friends jumped off the Brooklyn Bridge, would you jump too?

*

Only girls play with dolls.

*

So you think you're smart, do you?

*

Not now.

7

Retirement Quiz

Q: Why are retirees so slow to clean out the basement, attic, or garage?

A: They know as soon as they do, one of their adult kids will ask to store stuff there.

*

Q: What do retirees call a long lunch?

A: Normal.

*

Q: What's the difference between a birdhouse built by a Cub Scout and a birdhouse built by a retiree?

A: Three weeks, 17 trips to the hardware store, and about 1500 dollars worth of power tools.

*

Q: What's the only difference between recently married retirees and teenage newly-weds?

A: Fifty years.

*

Q: What most amazes new retirees?

A: They're so busy now, they don't know how they ever had time for work.

*

Q: What's the difference between a worker starting retirement and a young student starting summer vacation?

A: Summer ends.

*

Q: What's the best way to describe retirement?

A: The coffee break that never ends.

*

Q: What's the advantage of going back to school as a retiree?

A: If you cut classes, no one calls your parents.

*

Q: Why does a retiree often say he doesn't miss the job but he misses the people he used to work with?

A: He's too polite to tell the whole truth.

*

Q: Why don't retirees protest the stereotype that says they're either hyperactive or always napping?

A: They're either too busy to care what other people say, or they're asleep.

*

Q: Why don't retirees mind being called "senior citizens"?

A: The term comes with a ten percent discount.

*

Q: When is a retiree's bedtime?

A: Three hours after he falls asleep on the sofa watching TV.

*

Q: How many retirees does it take to change a lightbulb?

A: Only one, but it might take all day.

*

Q: What's the biggest complaint among retirees?

A: There's not enough time to get everything done.

*

Q: Among retirees, what's considered formal attire?

A: Tied shoes.

*

Q: Why do retirees count pennies?

A: They're the only ones who have the time.

*

Q: What's the common term for someone who enjoys her work so much she refuses to retire?

A: Nuts.

*

Q: What's the biggest advantage of retiring at age 62?

A: Not working at age 63.

8

Maturity

Age is a high price to pay for maturity.

Tom Stoppard

*

Maturity is the ability to do a job whether or not you are supervised, to carry money without spending it, and to bear an injustice without wanting to get even.

Ann Landers

*

Maturity begins when we're content to feel we're right about something without feeling the necessity to prove someone else wrong.

Sydney J. Harris

*

Maturity is reached the day we don't need to be lied to about anything.

Frank Yerby

*

Youth is when you blame all your troubles on your parents; maturity is when you learn that everything is the fault of the younger generation.

Harold Coffin

9
Nostalgia

Nostalgia is a file that removes the rough edges from the good old days.

Doug Larson

*

Nostalgia consists of longing for the place you wouldn't move back to.

Russ Fisher

*

People seem to get nostalgic about a lot of things they weren't so crazy about the first time around.

*

Nostalgia is a longing for something you couldn't stand anymore.

Fibber McGee (Jim Jordan)

*

A trip to nostalgia now and then is good for the spirit, as long as you don't set up housekeeping.

Dan Bartolovic

10

Old Age Happens When...

Old age happens when...the skin under your biceps flaps in the breeze.

*

Old age happens when...you hear the term "CD" and you think "certificate of deposit," not "compact disc."

*

Old age happens when...you're beginning to find polyester more appealing.

*

Old age happens when...the little gray-haired old lady you help across the street is your wife.

*

Old age happens when...you find it's easier to pick your teeth now—just take them out of your mouth and hold them up to the light.

*

Old age happens when...people start cutting your meat for you.

*

Old age happens when...all your enemies are dead.

*

Old age happens when...you no longer laugh at guys wearing white shoes or white belts.

*

Old age happens when...you get into a heated argument about pension plans.

*

Old age happens when...the flight attendant helps you put your bag in the overhead compartment.

*

Old age happens when...you don't care if your spouse puts the cap back on the Poli-Grip after each use.

❋

Old age happens when...actions creak louder than words.

❋

Old age happens when...you get out of the shower and you're glad the mirror is all fogged up.

❋

Old age happens when...you are suddenly receiving more "get well" cards than junk mail.

❋

Old age happens when...you feel bad in the morning without having had any fun the night before.

❋

Old age happens when...you look forward to receiving the AARP magazine.

❋

Old age happens when...all you talk about is your operation.

❋

Old age happens when...you start obsessing over who'll die first: you or your money.

*

Old age happens when...you sit in a rocking chair and can't get the darned thing going.

*

Old age happens when...you'll never have to go in-line skating.

*

Old age happens when...everyone refers to you as statuesque, settled, stately, spry, active, majestic, vigorous, or well-preserved.

*

Old age happens when...bingo becomes a spectator sport.

*

Old age happens when...your greatest exercise is feeding pigeons.

*

Old age happens when...your passions have turned to pensions.

*

Old age happens when...the toilet has become one of your favorite inventions.

*

Old age happens when...with-it teens
think your blue hair is cool.

11

Name the Year Quiz—
The 1940s

1.   What Year Was It? _____

The song: "Anchors Aweigh"

World War II ends with the dropping of the atomic bombs on Hiroshima and Nagasaki

The fads include Eisenhower jackets, bubble gum, crew cuts, and pageboy hairstyles

The movie: *The Lost Weekend*

The new look was full, calf-length skirts with tight waists

*

2.   What Year Was It? _____

Cole Porter's *Kiss Me Kate*

The play: *Death of a Salesman*

The song: "Rudolph the Red-Nosed Reindeer"

The samba becomes popular

Milton Berle hosts the first telethon

*

3.   What Year Was It? _____

The Selective Service Act

The Pasadena Freeway becomes the first freeway in the United States

NBC broadcasts its first official television program

The movie: *Grapes of Wrath*

*

4.   What Year Was It? _____

The GI Bill helps to educate millions

The movie: *Going My Way*

The song: "Swinging on a Star"

The song: "Have Yourself a Merry Little Christmas"

*

5.   What Year Was It? _____

The song: "Zip-a-dee-doo-dah"

Anne Frank: *The Diary of a Young Girl*

NBC launches "Meet the Press"

The CIA is formed

"Howdy Doody" becomes a hit

*

6.   What Year Was It? _____

The movie: *Citizen Kane*

Toy balloons and toy boats become popular

Rogers and Hart: "Bewitched, Bothered, and Bewildered"

The songs: "Deep in the Heart of Texas" and "Chattanooga Choo-Choo"

*

7.   What Year Was It? _____

U.S. income tax withholding begins

Rogers and Hammerstein: *Oklahoma*

The movie: *Casablanca*

U.S. polio epidemic

Zoot suits and the jitterbug become popular

*

8.   What Year Was It? _____

The song: "All I Want for Christmas Is My Two Front Teeth"

The movie: *A Streetcar Named Desire*

The movie: *Oliver Twist*

Alfred Kinsey: *Sexual Behavior in the American Male*

Nestlé's Quik is introduced

*

9.   What Year Was It? _____

The musical: *Annie Get Your Gun*

The Dead Sea scrolls discovered

Bugsy Siegel opens the first resort casino, the Flamingo Hotel, in Las Vegas

Dr. Benjamin Spock's *Baby and Child Care*

*

10. What Year Was It? _____

Frank Sinatra electrifies fans

"White Christmas" by Bing Crosby becomes the number-one song

The movie: *Bambi*

Americans face wartime shortages of coffee, sugar, and gasoline

*

Answers
1. 1945 2. 1949 3. 1940 4. 1944 5. 1947
6. 1941 7. 1943 8. 1948 9. 1946 10. 1942

12

Oldies But Goodies

Let us so live that when we come to die even the undertaker will be sorry.

Mark Twain

*

My dad's pants kept creeping up on him. By 65 he was just a pair of pants and a head.

Jeff Altman

*

Better a little "taffy" while they are living than so much "epitaphy" when they're dead.

*

Doctor: You should live to be 80.
Patient: I'm 85.
Doctor: See, what did I tell you!

*

I heard my wife telling the neighbor that I was a model husband. I felt pretty good until I looked up the word in the dictionary: "A model is a small imitation of the real thing."

*

Thirty-five is a very attractive age. London society is full of women of the very highest birth who have, of their own free choice, remained 35 for years.

*

Minor operation: Any operation that someone else has.

*

She may very well pass for 43 in the dusk with a light behind her!

W. S. Gilbert

*

Looking 50 is great—if you're 60.

Joan Rivers

*

I am prepared to meet my Maker. Whether my Maker is prepared for the ordeal of meeting me is another matter.

Winston Churchill

*

The seven ages of man: spills, drills, thrills, bills, ills, pills, wills.

Richard J. Needham

＊

Age is nothing but experience, and some of us are more experienced than others.

Andy Rooney

＊

I can't tell you his age, but when he was born the wonder drug was Mercurochrome.

＊

He's so old he has a digital sundial!

＊

An archaeologist is the best husband a woman can have; the older she gets, the more interested he is in her.

Agatha Christie

＊

As we grow older, our bodies get shorter and our anecdotes longer.

Robert Quillen

＊

Just remember, when you're over the hill, you begin to pick up speed.

Charles Schulz

*

Don McNeill tells about the woman who was filling out an application for credit. When she came to the space for age, she hesitated a long time. Finally the clerk leaned over and said, "The longer you wait, the worse it gets."

*

Once you get to be 100, you have made it. You almost never hear of anyone dying who is over 100.

George Burns

*

Old age is creaking up on her!

*

An elderly lady who was asked by a child if she were young or old said, "My dear, I have been young a very long time."

*

Age is a relative thing: You're young as long as you have a relative who is older.

*

"How old are you?" When a census taker asked a certain woman this, she said, "Well, now, let me figure it out. I was 18 when I married, and my husband was 30. He is now 60, or twice as old as he was then, so I am now 36."

✳

The doctors said at the time that she couldn't live more than a fortnight, and she's been trying ever since to see if she could. Women are so opinionated.

Saki

✳

Supreme Court Justice Oliver Wendell Holmes, Jr., was out for a stroll in the park with a friend when a pretty young girl happened by. Mr. Holmes, near 90 years of age, turned to his friend and said, "Oh, what I'd give to be 70 again!"

✳

What on earth will today's younger generation be able to tell their children they had to do without?

✳

When a man has a birthday, he may try to take a day off. When a woman has a birthday, she'll try to take five years off.

*

It is said that most elephants have a longer life span than human beings. Mankind has been trying to determine the whys of this phenomenon. Maybe there is something to be said for working for peanuts. Then again, the elephant's long life may be the result of a thick skin.

*

Ken and Melba finished their breakfast at the retirement home and were relaxing in the library. "You know," said Melba, "today, in most marriage ceremonies, they don't use the word 'obey' anymore."

"Too bad, isn't it?" retorted Ken. "It used to lend a little humor to the occasion."

*

At 20 we don't care what the world thinks of us. At 30 we worry about what it thinks of us. At 60 we discover that it wasn't ever thinking of us.

Sam Levenson

*

A Baptist preacher was at the hospital visiting Aunt Suzie. She explained to him that she had all 16 of her teeth pulled at one time. She didn't have any teeth.

While the preacher was talking to her, he was eating peanuts that were in a bowl on the nightstand. He would talk and he would eat. He visited, then he got up and said, "Mrs. Mowers, I'll be back to see you tomorrow, and I'll bring you more peanuts."

She said, "No! No, I can't chew 'em. So don't bring me no peanuts till I get me some teeth. My gums are too tender now. What I do now is just suck the chocolate off them peanuts and put the peanuts back into the bowl right there."

*

An elderly lady driving a big, new, expensive car was preparing to back into a parallel parking space when suddenly a young man in a small sports car zoomed in ahead of her. The woman angrily asked why he had done that when he could tell she was trying to park there. His response was simply, "Because I'm young, and I'm quick." The young man then entered the store. When he came back out a few minutes later, he found the elderly lady using her big, new car as a battering ram, backing up, and then ramming it into his car. He very angrily asked her why she was wrecking his car. Her response was "Because I'm old, and I'm rich!"

13
Sage Advice

Few know how to be old.

La Rochefoucauld

*

When I was young I was amazed at Plutarch's statement that the elder Cato began at the age of 80 to learn Greek. I am amazed no longer. Old age is ready to undertake tasks that youth shirked because they would take too long.

W. Somerset Maugham

*

It is not by muscle, speed, or physical dexterity that great things are achieved, but by reflection, force of character, and judgment; in these qualities old age is usually not only not poorer, but is even richer.

Cicero

*

As a well-spent day brings happy sleep, so life well used brings happy death.

Leonardo da Vinci

*

Life is precious to the old person. He is not interested merely in thoughts of yesterday's good life and tomorrow's path to the grave. He does not want his later years to be a sentence of solitary confinement in society. Nor does he want them to be a death watch.

David Allman

*

What you learn in youth you do not unlearn in old age.

*

All one's life as a young woman one is on show, a focus of attention, people notice you. You set yourself up to be noticed and admired. And then, not expecting it, you become middle-aged and anonymous. No one notices you. You achieve a wonderful freedom, it is a positive thing. You can move about, unnoticed and invisible.

Doris Lessing

*

We ought not to heap reproaches on old age, seeing that we all hope to reach it.

Bion

*

It gives me great pleasure to converse with the aged. They have been over the road that all of us must travel, and know where it is rough and difficult and where it is level and easy.

Plato

*

I am long on ideas, but short on time. I expect to live to be only about a hundred.

Thomas A. Edison

*

Aging seems to be the only available way to live a long time.

Daniel François Esprit

*

There has never been an intelligent person of the age of 60 who would consent to live his life over again—his or anyone else's.

*

I'm over 80 in a world where the young reject the old with more intensity than ever before....Now I'd like my old age to be my best performance. Death is the best exit.

Maurice Chevalier

*

When I was young, I was told: "You'll see, when you're 50." I am 50 and I haven't seen a thing.

Erik Satie

*

I don't worry about getting old. I'm old already. Only young people worry about getting old. When I was 65 I had cupid's eczema. I don't believe in dying. It's been done. I'm working on a new exit. Besides, I can't die now—I'm booked.

George Burns

*

Life is what happens to you when you're busy making other plans.

John Lennon

*

If you live long enough, the venerability factor creeps in; you get accused of things you never did and praised for virtues you never had.

*

I am delighted to be with you. In fact, at my age, I am delighted to be anywhere.

*

I think we're finally at a point where we've learned to see death with a sense of humor. I have to. When you're my age, it's as if you're a car. First a tire blows, and you get that fixed. Then a headlight goes, and you get that fixed. And then one day, you drive into a shop and the man says, "Sorry, miss, they don't have this make anymore."

Katharine Hepburn

*

I'm not interested in age. People who tell me their age are silly. You're as old as you feel.

Elizabeth Arden

*

If you carry your childhood with you, you never become older.

Abraham Sutzkever

*

Sure, I'm for helping the elderly. I'm going to be old myself someday (spoken when she was in her eighties).

Lillian Carter

*

People grow old by deserting their ideals. Years may wrinkle your skin but to give up interest wrinkles the soul.

General Douglas MacArthur

*

This increase in the life span and in the number of our senior citizens presents this nation with increased opportunities: the opportunity to draw upon their skill and sagacity—and the opportunity to provide the respect and recognition they have earned. It is not enough for a great nation merely to have added new years to life—our objective must also be to add new life to those years.

John F. Kennedy

*

Lord, save us all from old age and broken health and a hope-tree that has lost the faculty of putting out blossoms.

*

Men grow old, pearls grow yellow; there is no cure for it.

✳

Somebody asked me the other day, "What do you do?" "I amuse myself by growing old," I replied. "It's a full-time job."

Paul Leautaud

✳

The illusion that times that were are better than those that are, has probably pervaded all ages.

Horace Greeley

✳

The life of Henry Bailey Little is a fascinating one. In 1953, he celebrated 55 years as president of the Institution for Savings in Newburyport. Respected by his board of directors, Little was asked to serve another term. Surprisingly, he declined, stating it was time for a younger man to assume the leadership.

"So what's the big deal?" you may ask. Well, Henry Bailey Little was 102 years old and the "younger man" chosen to take his place was William Black. Oh, yes, the young replacement was 83.

✳

Some folks as they grow older grow wise, but most folks simply grow stubborner.

Josh Billings

14

Great Lies Out of Your Past

You don't look a day over 40.

*

If it will make you happy, it will make me happy.

*

It was delicious, but I couldn't eat another bite.

*

I'll call you later.

*

Of course I love you.

*

We only had three days' rain here last summer.

*

All our work is guaranteed.

*

I never received your fax.

*

You don't need it in writing—you have my word.

*

Trust me.

*

You must both come again.

*

Don't worry, I can go another 20 miles when the gauge is on empty.

*

The puppy won't be any trouble, Mom—I promise I'll look after it myself.

*

The truckers always know the best places to eat.

*

Your hair looks just fine.

*

It won't shrink in the wash.

*

I never inhaled.

*

My wife doesn't understand me.

*

The color really suits you.

*

It'll be as good as new.

*

But we can still be friends.

*

Don't worry, he's never bitten anyone.

*

The check is in the mail.

*

Having a great time. Wish you were here.

*

It's a very small spot—nobody will notice.

＊

It's supposed to make that noise.

＊

Come on, tell me. I promise I won't get angry.

＊

Now, I'm going to tell you the truth.

＊

The river never gets high enough to flood this property.

＊

I gave at the office.

＊

The new ownership won't affect you: The company will remain the same.

＊

It's not the money, it's the principle of the thing.

＊

The government will not raise taxes.

15
Old-Timers

I'm not getting old. My mirror is just getting wrinkled.

*

A man's life is 20 years of having his mother ask him where he is going, 40 years of having his wife ask the same question and, at the end, perhaps having the mourners wondering too.

*

We can't reach old age by another man's road. My habits protect my life, but they would assassinate you.

*

Anonymous prayer: Lord, Thou knowest better than I know myself that I am growing older. Keep me from getting too talkative, and thinking I must say something on every subject and on every occasion. Release me from craving to straighten out everybody's affairs. Teach me the glorious lesson that occasionally it is possible that I may be mistaken. Make me thoughtful, but not moody; helpful, but not bossy; for Thou knowest, Lord, that I want a few friends at the end.

✱

Growing old is like being increasingly penalized for a crime you haven't committed.

✱

Old people are fond of giving good advice; it consoles them for no longer being capable of setting a bad example.

✱

As I grow old, I find myself less and less inclined to take the stairs two at a time.

✱

Old age does not announce itself.

✱

Old age is like everything else. To make a success of it, you've got to start young.

Fred Astaire

✱

To be 70 years old is like climbing the Alps. You reach a snow-crowned summit, and see behind you the deep valley stretching miles and miles away, and before you other summits higher and whiter, which you may have strength to climb, or may not. Then you sit down and meditate and wonder which it will be.

Henry Wadsworth Longfellow

✳

Enjoy the little things, for one day you may look back and realize they were the big things.

Robert Brault

✳

When women pass 30, they first forget their age; when 40, they forget that they ever remembered it.

Ninon de Lenclos

✳

Have you not a moist eye? a dry hand? a yellow cheek? a white beard? a decreasing leg? an increasing belly? Is not your voice broken? your wind short? your chin double? your wit single? and every part about you blasted with antiquity?

William Shakespeare

✳

In aging, the mind grows constipated and thick.

Montaigne

*

My Uncle Pat, he reads the death column every morning in the paper. And he can't understand how people always die in alphabetical order.

Hal Roach

*

As a white candle
In a holy place,
So is the beauty
Of an aged face.

*

My birthday! How many years ago? Twenty or 30? Don't ask me! Forty or 50? How can I tell? I do not remember my birth, you see!

Julia C. Dorr

A man is as old as he's feeling, a woman as old as she looks.

Mortimer Collins

*

I haven't asked you to make me young again. All I want is to go on getting older.

Konrad Adenauer

*

God, keep my heart attuned to laughter
When youth is done;
When all the days are gray days, coming after
The warmth, the sun.
God, keep me then from bitterness, from grieving,
When life seems cold;
God, keep me always loving and believing
As I grow old.
A little more tired at close of day,
A little less anxious to have our way;
A little less ready to scold and blame;
A little more care of a brother's name;
And so we are nearing the journey's end,
Where time and eternity meet and blend.

Rollin J. Wells

*

You may search my time-worn face,
You'll find a merry eye that twinkles.
I am NOT an old lady
Just a little girl with wrinkles!

*

Who Wrote Whom?
Just a line to say I'm living,
that I'm not among the dead.
Though I'm getting more forgetful

and mixed up in the head.
I got used to my arthritis,
to my dentures I'm resigned.
I can manage my bifocals,
but I sure do miss my mind.
For sometimes I can't remember
when I stand at the foot of the stairs,
If I must go up for something,
or have I just come down from there?

16

Bald Is Beautiful

He never worried about his baldness. He was born that way!

*

If he had stopped at five foot six, he would have had no problem....Unfortunately, when he shot up to six foot, he went straight through his hair!

*

Frank is very upset and frustrated tonight; he spent 40 minutes blow-drying his hair and then forgot to bring it with him!

*

His hair was as white as snow, but somebody shoveled it off!

*

This guy is living proof that it's not only tough at the top, it's shiny too.

*

Every week, he goes out looking for the perfect toupee. I call it his "Hairtrek"...he baldly goes where no man has baldly gone before.

*

Why does he buy such cheap toupees? Now he's starting to lose hair that isn't even his!

*

His hair is a new color: platinum bald.

*

The most delightful advantage of being bald: One can hear snowflakes.

*

The only thing that stops hair falling...is a floor.

*

The advantage of having a toupee is that you can go see a movie while your hair is being shampooed!

*

Over-the-hill men frequently worry about going bald and being forced to wear a toupee.

*

These days, most people try to put fiber into their diet. Bob Johnson likes to put fiber on top of his head!

*

I'll say this for him…that wig he's wearing makes him look 20 years sillier.

*

The older a man gets, the more ways he learns to part his hair. Some men pull what little bit of hair they have around on their head to cover their baldness. However, as a man gets even older, he realizes there are basically only three ways to wear your hair: parted, unparted, and departed.

*

At a college reunion, 30 years after graduation, one man said to another, "See that fellow over there? Well, he's gotten so bald and so fat he didn't even recognize me!"

*

He once had very wavy hair. Now he's only got beach left.

*

It's not that he's bald. It's just that his part won't quit.

*

You wish you also had the courage to be a bald man with a ponytail.

17

Do You Remember...

Do you remember...the hokey pokey?

*

Do you remember...the recipe for Nestlé's original Tollhouse cookies?

*

Do you remember...what a cowcatcher is?

*

Do you remember...when you were growing up, milk was delivered to your house, and the milkman would give you ice chips in the summer?

*

Do you remember...when you were a kid, you could eat your Halloween candy without inspecting it for pins?

*

Do you remember...when stores were closed on Sunday?

*

Do you remember…when you owned two cars that cost more than your first house?

*

Do you remember…when you used to pledge allegiance to a flag that had 48 stars?

*

Do you remember…the bouffant?

*

Do you remember…parents speaking another language in the house when they didn't want you to understand what they were saying?

*

Do you remember…circling what you wanted to watch in TV Guide?

*

Do you remember…inkwells?

*

Do you remember…acne?

*

Do you remember...when you could promise a child the moon without having to buy a space suit?

*

Do you remember...Michael Landon as "Little Joe"?

*

Do you remember...having fond memories of your hula hoop?

*

Do you remember...you once owned a baseball card that would be worth more than 5000 dollars today?

*

Do you remember...when people still snickered at the concept of bottled water?

*

Do you remember...a little bit of recreational property you had your eye on for so many years that is now part of the supermall parking lot?

✳

Do you remember…seeing Elvis on *The Ed Sullivan Show?*

✳

Do you remember…"Here's the church and here's the steeple, open the doors and see all the people"?

✳

Do you remember…you had a big crush on Annette?

✳

Do you remember…being a blackboard monitor and clapping erasers?

✳

Do you remember…some of the verses to "Davy Crockett"?

✳

Do you remember…you used to say "far out"?

✳

Do you remember…putting "Kick Me" on the back of your friends' shirts?

*

Do you remember...as a kid, you wanted freckles. Now you have them—and they're big.

*

Do you remember...when it cost more to run a car than to park it?

*

Do you remember...sitting on a phone book at the dinner table?

*

Do you remember...you knew who J.F.K. was before the Oliver Stone movie came out?

18

Midlife Crisis

Being middle-aged is a nice change from being young.

Dorothy Canfield Fisher

*

Of the few innocent pleasures left to men past middle life, the jamming of common sense down the throats of fools is perhaps the keenest.

T. H. Huxley

*

Youth is when you're allowed to stay up late on New Year's Eve. Middle age is when you're forced to.

Bill Vaughan

*

Middle age is the awkward period when Father Time starts catching up with Mother Nature.

Harold Coffin

*

In youth, everything seems possible, but we reach a point in the middle years when we realize that we are never going to reach all the shining goals we had set for ourselves. And in the end, most of us reconcile ourselves, with what grace we can, to living with our ulcers and arthritis, our sense of partial failure, our less-than-ideal families—and even our politicians!

Adlai E. Stevenson

*

Middle age is when the only thing that can lead you down the garden path is a seed catalog.

Ivern Boyett

*

Midlife crisis is that moment when you realize your children and your clothes are about the same age.

Bill Tammeus

*

Middle age is when skintight isn't that accurate a description.

Robert Orben

*

Middle age is when anything new in the way you feel is most likely a symptom.

Laurence J. Peter

*

Middle age is when you have met so many people that every new person you meet reminds you of someone else and usually is.

Ogden Nash

*

In a man's middle years there is scarcely a part of the body he would hesitate to turn over to the proper authorities.

E. B. White

*

Middle age is when you begin to exchange your emotions for symptoms.

Irvin Shrewsbury Cobb

*

Whoever, in middle age, attempts to realize the wishes and hopes of his early youth invariably deceives himself. Each ten years of a man's life has its own fortunes, its own hopes, its own desires.

Goethe

19
Name the Year Quiz—
The 1950s

1.   What Year Was It? _____

Rogers and Hammerstein: *The King and I*

The first color TV set

I Love Lucy debuts

7-Up is introduced

The movie: *The African Queen*

The Roy Rogers Show premieres on NBC

*

2.   What Year Was It? _____

Frank Sinatra's *Come Dance with Me* album

The play: *The Miracle Worker*

Ben-Hur becomes the top movie

Barbie dolls debut

The movie: *Anatomy of a Murder*

*

3.   What Year Was It? _____

The song: "A Bushel and a Peck"

Ray Bradbury writes *The Martian Chronicles*

The Diners Club Card becomes the first nationally recognized credit card

Thirty-three million dollars is stolen in the Brinks robbery

Mr. Potato Head debuts

*

4.   What Year Was It? _____

Disneyland becomes the world's first theme park

Ray Kroc creates McDonald's

The Lawrence Welk Show premieres on ABC

Gunsmoke begins a 20-year TV run

Ann Landers begins giving advice

*

5.   What Year Was It? _____

The first bank credit card

The Today Show begins

The movie: *High Noon*

Steinbeck writes *East of Eden*

The song: "I Saw Mommy Kissing Santa Claus"

*

6.   What Year Was It? _____

Dr. Seuss: *The Cat in the Hat*

Leave It to Beaver premieres on CBS

The movie: *The Bridge on the River Kwai*

USSR launches Sputniks I, II

Beatniks become popular

*

7.   What Year Was It? _____

The movie: *From Here to Eternity*

Bikinis, petticoats, head scarves, and jeans become fads

Frisbees are introduced

Patty Paige sings "Doggie in the Window"

GM introduces the Chevrolet Corvette

*

8.   What Year Was It? _____

78 rpm records discontinue

Elvis sings "Jailhouse Rock" and "King Creole"

Hula hoops make their debut

Phone-booth stuffing becomes a fad

The movie: *Gigi*

Elvis appears in *Loving You, Jailhouse Rock,* and *King Creole*

*

9.   What Year Was It? _____

Elvis Presley's first major single: "Heartbreak Hotel"

The movie: *The Ten Commandments*

Sabin develops oral polio vaccine

Grace Kelley marries Prince Rainier of Monaco

Seat belts are added to cars

*

10. What Year Was It? _____

"Rock Around the Clock" by Bill Haley and the Comets

The movie: *Three Coins in the Fountain*

Tolkien: *Lord of the Rings*

Swanson TV dinner debuts

Howard Johnson's becomes the first hotel chain

The Tonight Show debuts on NBC

Answers
1. 1951 2. 1959 3. 1950 4. 1955 5. 1952
6. 1957 7. 1953 8. 1958 9. 1956 10. 1954

20

The Search for Happiness

The U.S. Constitution doesn't guarantee happiness, only the pursuit of it. You have to catch up with it yourself.

Benjamin Franklin

*

To be busy is man's only happiness.

Mark Twain

*

Never mind your happiness; do your duty.

Will Durant

*

There is only one way to happiness, and that is to cease worrying about things which are beyond the power of our will.

Epictetus

*

We are all happy, if we only knew it.

Fyodor Dostoyevsky

*

True happiness…is not attained through self-gratification, but through fidelity to a worthy purpose.

Helen Keller

*

In about the same degree as you are helpful, you will be happy.

Karl Reiland

*

The really happy man is one who can enjoy the scenery on a detour.

*

It isn't our position, but our disposition, that makes us happy.

*

One thing I know: The only ones among you who will be really happy are those who will have sought and found how to serve.

Albert Schweitzer

*

It is comparison that makes men happy or miserable.

*

When one door of happiness closes another opens; but often we look so long at the closed door that we do not see the one which has been opened for us.

Helen Keller

*

If I were to suggest a general rule for happiness, I would say, "Work a little harder; work a little longer; work!"

Frederick H. Ecker

*

Scatter seeds of kindness everywhere you go;

Scatter bits of courtesy—watch them grow and grow.

Gather buds of friendship, keep them till full-blown;

You will find more happiness than you have ever known.

Amy R. Raabe

*

We cannot hold a torch to light another's path without brightening our own.

Ben Sweetland

*

Happiness is like a cat. If you try to coax it or call it, it will avoid you. It will never come. But if you pay no attention to it and go about your business, you'll find it rubbing against your legs and jumping into your lap.

William Bennett

*

Happiness is the natural flower of duty.

Phillips Brooks

*

We have no more right to consume happiness without producing it than to consume wealth without producing it.

George Bernard Shaw

*

No man is happy unless he believes he is.

Publilius Syrus

*

To be happy we must not be too concerned with others.

Albert Camus

*

Just think how happy you would be if you lost everything you have right now—and then got it back again.

*

Happiness walks on busy feet.

Kitte Turmell

*

The search for happiness is one of the chief sources of unhappiness.

Eric Hoffer

*

The greatest happiness you can have is knowing that you do not necessarily require happiness.

William Saroyan

*

One is never as unhappy as one thinks, nor as happy as one hopes.

La Rochefoucauld

*

Recipe for happiness: Take equal parts of faith and courage, mix well with a sense of humor, sprinkle with a few tears, and add a helping of kindness for others. Bake in a good-natured oven and dust with laughter. Scrape away any self-indulgence that is apparent and serve with generous helpings.

*

The happiest people are rarely the richest, or the most beautiful, or even the most talented. Happy people do not depend on excitement and "fun" supplied by externals. They enjoy the fundamental, often very simple, things of life. They waste no time thinking other pastures are greener; they do not yearn for yesterday or tomorrow. They savor the moment, glad to be alive, enjoying their work, their families, the good things around them. They are adaptable; they can bend with the wind, adjust to the changes in their times, enjoy the contests of life, and feel themselves in harmony with the world. Their eyes are turned outward; they are aware, compassionate. They have the capacity to love.

Jane Canfield

*

Happiness sneaks in through a door you didn't know you left open.

*

One is never as fortunate or as unfortunate as one imagines.

La Rochefoucauld

*

The greatest discovery of any generation is that human beings can alter their lives by altering their attitudes.

Albert Schweitzer

*

Hours are happiest when hands are busiest.

*

Happiness is a habit—cultivate it.

Elbert Hubbard

*

All the art of living lies in a fine mingling of letting go and holding on.

Havelock Ellis

*

Happiness, I have discovered, is nearly always a rebound from hard work.

David Grayson

*

Don't be afraid to go out on a limb. That's where the fruit is.

H. Jackson Brown

*

Nine requisites for contented living:

Health enough to make work a pleasure. Wealth enough to support your needs. Strength to battle with difficulties and overcome them. Grace enough to confess your sins and forsake them. Patience enough to toil until some good is accomplished. Charity enough to see some good in your neighbor. Love enough to move you to be useful and helpful to others. Faith enough to make real the things of God. Hope enough to remove all anxious fears concerning the future.

Goethe

21

You're Getting Older
When You Remember...

You're getting older when you're the only one at the office who knows what a typewriter bell sounds like and which side of the carbon paper faces up.

✳

You're getting older when you remember how to do the bunny hop.

✳

You're getting older when you remember exactly where you were on November 22, 1963.

✳

You're getting older when you remember who Sergeant Bilko was.

✳

You're getting older when you remember attending a 3-D movie back when everyone really liked the cardboard eyeglasses they passed out in the lobby.

*

You're getting older when you remember
you once owned a coonskin cap.

*

You're getting older when you remember
wanting to be a rebel without a cause.

*

You're getting older when you remember
galoshes with big buckles.

*

You're getting older when you remember
making book covers out of brown paper bags.

*

You're getting older when you remember
learning penmanship.

*

You're getting older when you remember
meatless Tuesdays and Rosie the Riveter.

*

You're getting older when you remember
Tuesday nights with Uncle Miltie.

*

You're getting older when you remember making balsa wood model airplanes.

*

You're getting older when you remember making pipe-cleaner people and soapbox racers.

*

You're getting older when you remember making rubber-band guns.

*

You're getting older when you remember running boards.

*

You're getting older when you remember crepe paper.

*

You're getting older when you remember bellywopping.

*

You're getting older when you remember wearing cigar-band rings.

*

You're getting older when you remember cellophane.

*

You're getting older when you remember eating something without knowing how many calories it had, or caring, or even knowing what a calorie was.

*

You're getting older when you remember the boogie-woogie.

*

You're getting older when you remember being happy with a little box of raisins.

*

You're getting older when you remember getting into a car and going on a Sunday afternoon drive with your family.

*

You're getting older when you remember driving a DeSoto.

*

You're getting older when you remember saying words like *girdle, bobby sox,* and *Fred Waring*.

*

You're getting older when you remember you considered brown sugar on your oatmeal a real treat.

22
Smiles

Age is not important unless you're a cheese.

Helen Hayes

*

He's a remarkable gentleman…even at his age, he's still quite capable of putting away five or six pints a night…only prune juice, but…

*

My doctor gave me two weeks to live. I hope they're in August.

Ronnie Shakes

*

I don't have wrinkles. Those are laugh lines. I guess I do a lot of laughing.

*

It's a sign of age if you feel like the morning after the night before and you haven't been anywhere.

*

As one cat said to another: Birthdays are like fur balls—the more you have, the more you gag.

Marla Morgan

*

People often ask, "What's new?" I've come to that stage in life when if anything's new it's apt to be a symptom.

Lloyd Cory

*

The years between 50 and 70 are the hardest. You are always asked to do things, and you are not yet decrepit enough to turn them down.

T. S. Eliot

*

There's no use trying to get younger. A fellow'd better just try to keep on getting older.

Frank Clark

*

A man is as old as he feels. A woman is as old as she likes.

*

Seventy is wormwood
Seventy is gall
But it's better to be seventy
Than not alive at all.

Phyllis McGinley

*

You can stay young indefinitely if you eat wisely, get plenty of sleep, work hard, have a positive mental outlook, and lie about your age.

*

I'm saving up for my old age: arthritis, bursitis, cataracts...

*

The other night, while lying on a couch, I reviewed the high point of my life and fell asleep!

*

The age of some women is like the odometer on a used car—you know it's set back, but you don't know how far.

*

At 88 how do you feel when getting up in the morning? Amazed!

Ludwig von Mises

＊

They tell you that you'll lose your mind when you grow older. What they don't tell you is that you won't miss it very much.

Malcolm Cowley

＊

If you're yearning for the good old days, just turn off the air conditioning.

Griff Niblack

＊

In ancient times a woman was considered old at the age of 40. Today a woman of that age is only 29.

＊

You are as young as you feel after trying to prove it.

Lou Erickson

＊

A widow lived to be well into her nineties. On her birthdays, she always gave a little party for her friends and relatives, and they routinely brought her a small gift, such as a knick-knack for her apartment. One year, a friend phoned and asked, "What would you like for your birthday this year?"

"Oh, just give me a kiss," said the old woman. "Then I won't have to dust it."

✳

As for me, except for an occasional heart attack, I feel as young as I ever did.

Robert Benchley

✳

The age of 50 hit him so hard, he bounced all the way back to 43!

✳

I said to my old husband, "I'm gonna take you out into the country for a picnic. Do you like the country?" He said, "Sure I do. When I was a little boy, I used to live in the country." I said, "When you was a little boy *everybody* lived in the country."

Moms Mabley

✳

I've always wanted to be somebody, but I see now I should have been more specific.

Lily Tomlin

✳

"To what do you attribute your old age, Wilbur?" "I was born a long time ago!"

*

Ladies and gentlemen, Red Adair and his team are happy to announce that the candles on John MacArthur's birthday cake are now under control.

*

Two elderly ladies were sitting on a porch rocking back and forth in rocking chairs. "Sally," said one, "do you ever think about the hereafter?"

As quick as a flash, Sally replied, "All the time! I go into a room and look around and say, 'Now what was it I came in here after?'"

*

Jeffrey sneaked up behind a blue-haired beauty at a seniors' dance, covered her eyes with his hands, and said, "I'm going to kiss you, if you can't tell me who I am in three guesses."

"Teddy Roosevelt! Andrew Jackson! Abraham Lincoln!" she answered quickly.

*

My wife bought a new line of expensive cosmetics guaranteed to make her look years younger. After a lengthy sitting before the mirror applying the "miracle" products, she asked, "Darling, honestly what age would you say I am?"

Looking her over carefully, I replied, "Judging from your skin, 20; your hair, 18; and your figure, 25."

"Oh, you flatterer!" she gushed.

"Hey, wait a minute!" I interrupted. "I haven't added them up yet."

*

First I was dying to finish high school and start college. And then I was dying to finish college and start working. And then I was dying to marry and have children who grew old enough so I could return to work. And then I was dying to retire. And now, I am dying...and suddenly realize I forgot to live.

*

A man died and left his great wealth to his secretary. Naturally, his wife was furious. She went to have the inscription on his tombstone changed, but was too late. To change it now she would need to buy a new stone. She thought for a moment. She certainly didn't want to spend any more of her money, so she said, "Right after 'Rest in Peace' I want you to chisel in these additional words: 'Till We Meet Again.'"

*

An elderly gentleman on a train was mumbling to himself, smiling, and then raising his hand. After a moment of silence, he would go through the same process: mumble, smile, raise hand, silence.

Another passenger observed this, and after about an hour, he said, "Pardon me, sir. Is anything wrong?"

"Oh, no," replied the oldster. "It's just that long trips get boring so I tell myself jokes."

"But why, sir," asked the passenger, "do you keep raising your hand?"

"Well," said the oldster, "that's to interrupt myself because I've heard that one before."

23

Thoughts on Aging

Anyone who stops learning is old, whether at 20 or 80. Anyone who keeps learning stays young. The greatest thing in life is to keep your mind young.

Henry Ford

*

The older I get, the more wisdom I find in the ancient rule of taking first things first—a process which often reduces the most complex human problems to manageable proportions.

Dwight D. Eisenhower

*

The greatest compensation of old age is its freedom of spirit....Another compensation is that it liberates you from envy, hatred, and malice.

W. Somerset Maugham

*

I'm saving that rocker for the day when I feel as old as I really am.

Dwight D. Eisenhower

*

If it is the devil that tempts the young to enjoy themselves, is it not, perhaps, the same personage that persuades the old to condemn their enjoyment? And is not condemnation perhaps merely the form of excitement appropriate to old age?

Bertrand Russell

*

Live as long as you may, the first 20 years are the longest half of your life.

Robert Southey

*

Many foxes grow gray, but few grow good.

Benjamin Franklin

*

The essence of age is intellect.

Emerson

*

It does not become an old man to run after the fashion of the moment, either in thought or in dress. But he should know where he is, and what the others are aiming at.

Goethe

*

The older I grow, the more I listen to people who don't talk much.

Germain G. Glidden

*

The ultimate test of man's conscience may be his willingness to sacrifice something today for future generations whose words of thanks will not be heard.

Gaylord Nelson

*

A man must have grown old and lived long in order to see how short life is.

Schopenhauer

*

If you carry your childhood with you, you never become older.

Abraham Sutzkever

*

Growing up is usually so painful that people make comedies out of it to soften the memory.

John Greenwald

*

People often say that this or that person has not yet found himself. But the self is not something that one finds. It is something one creates.

Thomas Szasz

*

Wisdom doesn't necessarily come with age. Sometimes age just shows up all by itself.

Tom Wilson

*

You can clutch the past so tightly to your chest that it leaves your arms too full to embrace the present.

Jan Glidewell

*

When I was young, I admired clever people. Now that I am old, I admire kind people.

Abraham Joshua Heschel

*

You are young at any age if you are planning for tomorrow.

*

You cannot do a kindness too soon, for you never know how soon it will be too late.

Ralph Waldo Emerson

*

The older you get, the more important it is not to act your age.

Ashleigh Brilliant

*

You can judge your age by the amount of pain you feel when you come in contact with a new idea.

John Nuveen

*

Keep some souvenirs of your past, or how will you ever prove it wasn't all a dream?

Ashleigh Brilliant

*

You grow up the day you have your first real laugh—at yourself.

Ethel Barrymore

*

You're never too old to grow up.

Shirley Conran

*

Nothing in life is to be feared. It is only to be understood.

Marie Curie

*

As we grow old, the beauty steals inward.

Ralph Waldo Emerson

*

The young man knows the rules, but the old man knows the exceptions.

Oliver Wendell Holmes Sr.

*

Time carries all things, even our wits, away.

Virgil

*

The misery of a child is interesting to a mother, the misery of a young man is interesting to a young woman, the misery of an old man is interesting to nobody.

Victor Hugo

24

You're Never Too Old

Neither Henry Ford nor Abraham Lincoln realized any success until after they were 40 years old.

*

George Burns won his first Oscar at 80.

*

Albert Schweitzer was still performing operations in his African hospital at 89.

*

Will and Ariel Durant wrote the massive ten-volume "History of Civilization" between the ages of 69 and 89.

*

Herbert Hoover, at 84, served as U.S. representative to Belgium.

*

Golda Meir was 71 when she became prime minister of Israel.

*

John D. Rockefeller was making one million dollars a week when he died at 93.

*

Arthur Fiedler conducted the Boston Pops orchestra in his eighties.

*

Grandma Moses painted over 1500 paintings. She started when she was 80 years old. Twenty-five percent of her paintings were painted after she was over 100 years old.

*

George Bernard Shaw was 94 when one of his plays was first produced. At 96, he broke his leg when he fell out of a tree he was trimming in his backyard.

*

Michelangelo was 71 when he painted the Sistine Chapel.

*

S. I. Hayakawa retired as president of San Francisco State University at 70, and was then elected to the U.S. Senate.

*

Ralph Vaughan Williams composed his eighth and ninth symphonies in his eighties.

*

Doc Counsilman, at 58, became the oldest person ever to swim the English Channel.

*

I will not make age an issue of this campaign. I am not going to exploit for political purposes my opponent's youth and inexperience. (Televised presidential debate with Walter Mondale, 1984; Reagan was 73, Mondale was 56.)

*

There is nothing more remarkable in the life of Socrates than that he found time in his old age to learn to dance and play on instruments, and thought it was time well spent.

Montaigne

*

Pablo Casals played the cello, conducted orchestras, and taught up to the time of his death at 96.

*

Casey Stengel didn't retire from the rigorous schedule of managing the New York Mets until he was 75.

*

Charlie Chaplin, at 76, was still directing movies.

*

Verdi composed "Ave Maria" at 85.

*

Gordie Howe remained a top competitor in the National Hockey League into his early fifties.

*

Benjamin Franklin had the honor of framing the U.S. Constitution when he was 81.

*

Winston Churchill assumed the role of Great Britain's prime minister at 65. At 70, he addressed the crowds on V-E Day, standing on top of his car to speak.

*

"It is too late!" Ah, nothing is too late—
Cato learned Greek at 80; Sophocles
wrote his grand "Oedipus," and Simonides
Bore off the prize of verse from his com-
peers
When each had numbered more than
fourscore years;
And Theophrastus, at fourscore and ten,
had begun his "Character of Men."
Chaucer, at Woodstock, with his nightin-
gales,
At 60 wrote the "Canterbury Tales."
Goethe, at Weimar, toiling to the last,
Completed "Faust" when 80 years were
past.
What then? Shall we sit idly down and say,
"The night has come; it is no longer day"?
For age is opportunity no less
Than youth itself, though in another
dress.
And as the evening twilight fades away,
The sky is filled with stars, invisible by day.
It is never too late to start doing what is
right.
Never.

Henry Wadsworth Longfellow

25

Name the Year Quiz— The 1960s

1. What Year Was It? _____

Chubby Checker introduces the Twist

"Georgia on My Mind" becomes a hit for Ray Charles

Oral contraceptives

The world population tops three billion

The movies: *Exodus* and *Psycho*

*

2. What Year Was It? _____

Frank Sinatra wins a Grammy for *Strangers in the Night*

The movies: *Who's Afraid of Virginia Woolf?* and *Fahrenheit 451*

The first Medicare ID card presented to Harry Truman

Mission Impossible premieres on CBS

Walt Disney dies

*

3.   What Year Was It? _____

The Beatles: "Hey Jude"

The movie: *2001: A Space Odyssey*

60 Minutes debuts

McDonalds introduces the Big Mac

Jackie Kennedy marries Aristotle Onassis

*

4.   What Year Was It? _____

The songs: "Moon River," "Blue Moon," and "Hit the Road, Jack"

The Peace Corps is created

The movie: *West Side Story*

Freedom Riders civil rights works attacked by whites

Soviet astronauts orbit earth

*

5.   What Year Was It? _____

Weight Watchers is founded

Alfred Hitchcock's *The Birds* hits the theaters

Patsy Cline killed in a plane crash

The Beatles sing "I Want to Hold Your Hand"

First-class postal rate is five cents

Dominos delivers its first pizza

*

6.   What Year Was It? _____

The song: "Blowin' in the Wind"

ABC begins color telecasts

Tab-opening cans make their debut

The first Wal-Mart store and the first Kmart store

Movie: *Lawrence of Arabia*

*

7.   What Year Was It? _____

Eight-track tapes debut

The Grateful Dead rock group forms

Diet Pepsi introduced

The movie: *The Sound of Music*

Haight-Ashbury becomes the center of the LSD and psychedelic movement

*

8.   What Year Was It? _____

Pop-Tarts toaster pastries introduced

G.I. Joe doll introduced

The popular dances are the Watusi, Frug, Monkey, and Funky Chicken

Elizabeth Taylor marries Richard Burton

The movies: *My Fair Lady, Mary Poppins,* and *Goldfinger*

*

9.   What Year Was It? _____

The Beatles: *Sergeant Pepper's Lonely Hearts Club Band*

Rolling Stones appear on the *Ed Sullivan Show*

The Twist, yogurt, miniskirts, turtlenecks, and Afro hairstyles catch on

The movie: *Bonnie and Clyde*

The movie: *Guess Who's Coming to Dinner?*

*

10. What Year Was It? _____

Sinatra records "My Way"

PBS launches *Sesame Street*

The movie: *Midnight Cowboy*

Woodstock music festival, where 300,000 listen to music and wallow in the mud

The movie: *Butch Cassidy and the Sundance Kid*

Neil Armstrong becomes the first person to walk on the moon

Answers

1. 1960 2. 1966 3. 1968 4. 1961 5. 1963
6. 1962 7. 1965 8. 1964 9. 1967 10. 1969

26
Underground Humor

Here lies the body of William Smith; and, what is somewhat rarish: He was born, bred, and hanged in this parish.

Penryn Cornwall

*

Owen Moore:
Gone away
Owin' more
Than he could pay

*

A baker retires:
Throughout his life
he kneaded bread
And deemed it quite a bore.
But now six feet beneath
earth's crust
He needeth bread no more.

*

Here lies Ann Mann
She lived an old maid
But died an old Mann

*

George S. Kaufman
(Suggestion for his own epitaph):
Over my dead body!

*

If the general had known how big a funeral he was going to have he would have died years ago.

Abraham Lincoln

*

Alfred Hitchcock: I'm involved in a plot.

*

In joyous memory of
George Jones who was president of
the Newport Rifle Club
for twenty years.
"Always missed."

*

Gravestone epitaph requested by Erma Bombeck:
Big deal! I'm used to dust.

*

This is the grave of Mike O'Day
Who died maintaining his right of way.
His right was clear, his will was strong.
But he's just as dead as if he'd been wrong.

*

They say such nice things about people at their funerals that it makes me sad to realize I'm going to miss mine by just a few days.

Garrison Keillor

*

Wherever you be
Let your wind go free.
For it was keeping it in
That was the death of me.

*

Under this stone, Reader, survey
Dead Sir John Vanbrugh's house of clay.
Lie heavy on him, Earth! for he
Laid many heavy loads on thee!

*

Beneath this silent tomb is laid
A noisy, antiquated maid;
Who from her cradle talked till death
And ne'er before was out of breath.

*

Here lies an honest lawyer—
That is Strange.
(on the gravestone of the eminent barrister, Sir John Strange)

*

He is a good man—according to his epitaph.

*

Here lies
Lester Moore
Four slugs from a 44
No Les
No More.

*

During a recent grave-digger's strike this sign appeared at the entrance of one cemetery: "Due to the strike, all grave digging for the duration will be done by a skeleton crew."

*

Here I lie bereft of breath
Because a cough carried me off;
Then a coffin they carried me off in.

*

Here lies Dr. Keene, the good Bishop of Chester,

Who ate up a fat goose, but could not digest her.

*

She lived with
Her husband
Fifty years
And died in the
Confident hope
of a better life.

*

Here Lies
Ezekial Aikle
Aged 102
The Good
Die Young

*

Once I wasn't
Then I was
Now I ain't again

*

A hard testimonial marks this man's grave:
Here lies a man who did no good,
And if he'd lived he never would;
Where he's gone or how he fares,
Nobody knows and nobody cares.

*

Here lies Bernard Lightfoot who
was accidentally killed in the
forty-fifth year of his age.
Erected by his grateful family.

*

Sacred to the memory
of Anthony Drake,
Who died for peace
and quietness' sake.
His wife was constantly
scolding and scoffing,
So he sought repose
in a 12-dollar coffin.

*

On a healthy man's life:

Here lies the body of
Samuel Procter,
Who lived and died without
a doctor.

*

Stranger, tread this ground with gravity
Dentist Brown is filling his last cavity.

*

I had a hunch something like this would
happen.

Fontaine Fox

27

More Famous
Family Phrases
of the Middle-Aged

You might hate the piano now, but when you're older you'll be glad I made you practice every day.

*

Lizards don't make good house pets.

*

Ain't ain't in the dictionary.

*

Maybe tomorrow.

*

My father would have killed me if I had pulled a stunt like that.

*

Your barn door's open.

✻

You kids have it too easy nowadays.

✻

What's wrong with you, anyway?

✻

I don't care what your friends do.

✻

Why don't you act your age? How old are you, anyway?

✻

As long as you live in my house, you'll live by my rules.

✻

"Hey" is for horses.

✻

It's too nice outside to sit in front of the TV set.

✻

When I say no, I mean no. Why? Because, that's why.

*

He's not good enough for you.

*

You call that noise "music"?

*

Big boys don't cry.

*

Don't ask so many dumb questions.

*

If you want it, you pay for it.

*

How can you be hungry? We ate five minutes ago.

*

You don't know enough to come in out of the rain.

*

I'm rubber, you're glue.

*

This is not a horses' stable; get your elbows off the table.

*

Young ladies don't climb trees.

*

This is your last warning.

*

What's so funny? Wipe that smile off your face.

*

Eat this; you'll like it.

*

Don't give me that malarkey.

*

You can't make me. It's a free country.

*

Don't come crying to me.

28

Grandparents

My grandmother's 90. She's dating. He's 93. It's going great. They never argue. They can't hear each other.

*

After Christmas vacation, a teacher asked her small pupils to write an account of how they spent their holidays. One boy wrote as follows:

"We always spend Christmas with Grandma and Grandpa. They used to live up here in a big red house, but Grandpa got retarded and they moved to Florida.

"They live in a place with a lot of retarded people. They live in tin huts. They ride big three wheel tricycles. They go to a big building they call a wrecked hall but it is fixed now. They play games there and do exercises, but they don't do them very good. There is a swimming pool and they go to it and just stand there in the water with their hats on. I guess they don't know how to swim."

❋

"Grandpa, why don't you get a hearing aid?" "Don't need it. I hear more now than I can understand!"

❋

Grandpa Phillips was caught unprepared by the Colorado cold spell last winter and complained to his grandson that he hadn't been able to sleep.

"Did your teeth chatter, Grandpa?"

"Dunno," he replied. "We didn't sleep together."

❋

Satisfied Grandmother: If she had it to do all over again, she would bypass children and just have grandchildren.

❋

The best way to antique your furniture is to have several grandchildren around.

❋

The passing years sure make me ponder why Gramps gets gray and Grandma gets blonder.

*

The quickest way for a grandparent to get a grandchild's attention is to sit down and look comfortable.

*

A grandfather on an airplane flight turned to the occupant in the next seat and said, "Have I told you about my grandchildren?"

"No," said the gentleman, "and I certainly do appreciate it!"

*

Grandmother: A baby-sitter who doesn't hang around the refrigerator.

*

Two youngsters were talking about their families, and one asked, "Why does your grandmother spend so much time reading the Bible?"

"I don't know," replied the other, "but I think she's cramming for her finals."

*

When my time comes to die, I want to go quietly and with dignity like my grandfather, and not screaming and roaring like his passengers.

*

My grandmother made dying her life's work.

*

A child's thoughts about grandparents:
My grandma used to bake cookies and stuff. But I guess she forgot how. Nobody cooks—they all go out to fast-food restaurants.

As you come into the park, there is a dollhouse with a man sitting in it. He watches all day, so they can't get out without him seeing them. They wear badges with their names on them. I guess they don't know who they are.

My grandpa and grandma worked hard all their lives and earned their retardment. I wish they would move back home, but I guess the man in the dollhouse won't let them out.

*

Headline: Grandmother of eight makes hole in one.

*

Your grandchildren will be impressed that you lived in the twentieth century.

*

My grandfather's a little forgetful, but he likes to give me advice. One day he took me aside and left me there.

*

Grandchildren don't make a man feel old; it's the knowledge that he's married to a grandmother.

29

You Know You're Growing Older When...

You know you're growing older when... someone compliments you on your snakeskin shoes and you are barefoot!

*

You know you're growing older when... you're convinced more people are mumbling these days.

*

You know you're growing older when... you need to rock forward and backward a couple of times to propel yourself out of a low, soft easy chair.

*

You know you're growing older when... you haven't changed the color of your hair or lipstick in five years.

*

You know you're growing older when...
you don't go anywhere without a toothpick in
your purse or pocket.

*

You know you're growing older when...
you let out an involuntary grunt when you get
up from the sofa.

*

You know you're growing older when...
you go out to dinner with friends and you cal-
culate who owes how much down to the last
penny.

*

You know you're growing older when...
you rejoice over how young Sean Connery
looked in his last movie.

*

You know you're growing older when...
you consider yourself in the prime of senility.

*

You know you're growing older when...
you're always looking for your glasses.

*

You know you're growing older when...
dialing long-distance wears you out.

*

You know you're growing older when...
your idea of living on the edge is trying a new
flavor of nonfat yogurt.

*

You know you're growing older when...
you're on your fourth dog.

*

You know you're growing older when...
you've noticed lately that old people really
aren't that old, but young people seem *awfully*
young.

*

You know you're growing older when...
you travel with an inflatable, doughnut-shaped
seat cushion.

*

You know you're growing older when...
you had to find a new dentist because yours
retired.

*

You know you're growing older when... you get winded gumming a mint.

*

You know you're growing older when... your favorite part of the newspaper is "Twenty-five years ago today."

*

You know you're growing older when... after making a turn onto the highway you drive for the next 100 miles with your blinker on.

*

You know you're growing older when... your children give you a curfew.

*

You know you're growing older when... you hear the phrase "hot flash" and you don't think "news bulletin."

*

You know you're growing older when... you look forward to bingo night.

*

You know you're growing older when...
you own a high-strung Chihuahua.

*

You know you're growing older when...
you enter a room to get something and can't
for the life of you remember what it was.

*

You know you're growing older when...
you find that revolving doors move much
faster now than when you were younger.

*

You know you're growing older when...
you get out of breath playing chess.

*

You know you're growing older when...
you have to stand halfway out of the phone
booth just to read the numbers to dial.

*

You know you're growing older when...
you start doing jigsaw puzzles again.

✳

You know you're growing older when...it takes you longer to touch up your roots.

✳

You know you're growing older when... you don't even consider changing a flat tire but immediately call AAA.

✳

You know you're growing older when... high fiber and constipation become dinner topics.

✳

You know you're growing older when...it takes a half hour each morning to wake up your leg.

✳

You know you're growing older when... you no longer need to have your color chart done—you're always winter.

✳

You know you're growing older when... household items common when you were a kid are now found in antique shops.

*

You know you're growing older when...
you look for discounts at elderhostels.

*

You know you're growing older when...
after years of asking your children to turn the
TV down, you are now asking them to turn it
up.

*

You know you're growing older when...it
takes you more time to recover than it did to
tire you out.

*

You know you're growing older when...
your arthritis makes you less likely to lose your
wedding ring.

*

You know you're growing older when...
you can throw away the Christmas decorations
that your children made in nursery school.

*

You know you're growing older when...
your high school reunions are less crowded
than they used to be.

*

You know you're growing older when...
you walk with your head held high because
you're trying to get used to your bifocals.

*

You know you're growing older when...
your idea of an early-bird dinner is lunch.

*

You know you're growing older when...
you don't like people interfering with your
schedule of watching *The Price Is Right*.

*

You know you're growing older when...
your shoe size increases and you decrease in
height.

*

You know you're growing older when...
you buy your first Craftmatic adjustable bed.

*

You know you're growing older when...
your ties are back in style.

*

You know you're growing older when…at noon you begin planning your wardrobe for the "early-bird special."

*

You know you're growing older when… you're thinking of buying a cemetery plot.

*

You know you're growing older when… you ask for a senior discount and no one questions if you're old enough.

30

Laughter Is Good Medicine

They say you shouldn't say nothing about the dead unless it's good. He's dead. Good.

Moms Mabley

*

To be mortal is not any means wholly disadvantageous. When I catch myself resenting not being immortal, I pull myself up short by asking whether I should really like the prospect of having to make out an annual income tax return for an infinite number of years ahead.

Arnold J. Toynbee

*

Aging isn't all bad. Think of the trouble many of us would be in if wrinkles hurt!

*

There's a simple secret for long life: Get to be a hundred and then be careful!

*

An obituary notice in a newspaper recounted the impressive rites of a funeral service and then noted: "A spectator slipped at the gravesite and broke his leg. The accident cast a cloud of gloom over the whole occasion."

*

By the time we've made it, we've had it.

Malcolm Forbes

*

At my age, when I order a three-minute egg, they ask for the money up front.

Milton Berle

*

She was 102. She didn't have wrinkles, she had pleats.

Dennis Wolfberg

*

Remember when we used to laugh at old people when we were young? Do you recall what was so funny?

*

An old-timer is one who remembers when we counted our blessings instead of our calories.

Kate M. Owney

*

A humorous old gent said he hoped to soon put all his aches in one casket.

*

It takes about ten years to get used to how old you are.

*

Growing old is mandatory; growing up is optional.

*

They're having an age problem. He won't act his, and she won't tell hers.

*

People had much rather be thought to look ill than old, because it is possible to recover from sickness, but there is no recovering from age.

*

I don't feel 80. In fact, I don't feel anything till noon. Then it's time for my nap.

*

It's hard to know just where one generation ends and the next one begins, but it's somewhere around 9 P.M.

*

Another candle on your cake? Well, that's no reason to pout. Be glad that you have strength enough to blow the candle out.

*

I've discovered the secret of eternal youth. I lie about my age.

Bob Hope

*

Don't think of yourself as a senior citizen. Think of yourself as a dropout from the school of hard knocks.

*

She still aims at youth, though she shot beyond it years ago.

Charles Dickens

✻

At 66 I am entering…the last phase of my active physical life. My body, on the move, resembles in sight and sound nothing so much as a bin-liner full of yogurt.

Stephen Fry

✻

The four stages of man are infancy, childhood, adolescence, and obsolescence.

Art Linkletter

✻

Life begins when the kids leave home and the dog dies.

✻

People who knew her 30 years ago say she still looks like she looked then—old!

✻

Mark Twain said wrinkles are where smiles used to be.

✻

Being an old maid is like death by drowning—a really delightful sensation after you cease to struggle.

*

The best birthdays of all are those that haven't arrived yet.

Robert Orben

*

Birthdays are nice to have, but when you think about it, too many of them will kill you! Still, I'm too young to worry about that.

*

No matter who you are, you only get a little slice of the world. Have you ever seen a hearse followed by a U-Haul?

Billy Graham

*

On their sixtieth wedding anniversary, a reporter came to interview them. "What big problems have you had in your marriage?" he asked the elderly woman.

"Well, there's really been only two: Pa and the fire."

"What do you mean, 'Pa and the fire'?" asked the reporter.

With a gleam in her eye, she explained, "When I paid too much attention to one, the other went out!"

*

Young Williams completed an examination of an elderly man. "Tell me," asked the MD, "do you suffer from arthritis?"

"Of course!" snarled the senior. "What else can I do with it?"

*

"My wife always lies about her age." "My Lisa never lies about her age. She just tells people she's as old as I am. Then she lies about my age."

*

An old lady went to a tombstone-cutter's office to order a stone for her husband's grave. After explaining that all she wanted was a small one with no frills, she told him to put the words "To My Husband" in a suitable place. When the stone was delivered, she saw to her horror this inscription: "To My Husband—In a Suitable Place."

*

He finally invested in a hearing aid after becoming virtually deaf. It was one of the invisible kinds.

"Well, how do you like your new hearing aid?" asked his doctor.

"I like it great. I've heard sounds in the last few weeks that I didn't know existed."

"Well, how does your family like your hearing aid?"

"Oh, nobody in my family knows I have it yet. Am I having a great time! I've changed my will three times in the last two weeks!"

31

Name the Year Quiz— The 1970s

1. What Year Was It? _____

Beverly Sills becomes director of the New York City Opera

Sony Walkman introduced

The movie *The Deer Hunter* wins an Academy Award

The hurricanes Frederick and David cause widespread damage

*

2. What Year Was It? _____

Elvis Presley dies

Oil flows through the Alaska pipeline

The Concorde begins flying between New York, London, and Paris

The movie: *Star Wars*

Groucho Marx dies

Disco dancing sweeps the country

*

3.   What Year Was It? _____

Postage increases to 13 cents for first-class mail

Atari becomes the video game rage

The movie *Jaws* becomes a blockbuster

Hot pants, punk look, wide neckties, and the preppy look catch on

Patty Hearst caught by the FBI

*

4.   What Year Was It? _____

Stevie Wonder wins Album of the Year Grammy

The movie: *Last Tango in Paris*

Oregon is the first state to decriminalize marijuana

Energy crisis created by Arab oil embargo

McDonalds introduces the Egg McMuffin

*

5.   What Year Was It? _____

The movies: *Catch-22* and *True Grit*

Janis Joplin dies of a heroin overdose

The "hippy" look is big

One-hundred-percent polyester dresses sell for 16 dollars

*

6.   What Year Was It? _____

VHS home video format

First New York City marathon

Charlie's Angels premieres on ABC

The movie: *Rocky*

Israeli commandos rescue 103 hostages held at Uganda's Entebbe airport

Legionnaires' disease strikes for the first time

*

7.   What Year Was It? _____

Solzhenitsyn is first published in the United States

The first stand-alone video game, Pong

Lego and Slinky catch on

The movies: *Cabaret* and *The Godfather*

*

8.   What Year Was It? _____

The movie: *The Buddy Holly Story*

David Berkowitz, "Son of Sam," receives life imprisonment for six murders

California voters approve Proposition 13 to cut property taxes 57 percent

The movie: *Grease*

Jim Jones and his followers commit mass suicide in Jonestown, Guyana, by drinking Kool-Aid spiked with cyanide

*

9. What Year Was It? _____

Reggae music becomes popular

"Streaking" becomes a fad in the United States

Crack cocaine hits the public consciousness

Kidnapped heiress Patty Hearst joins the Symbionese Liberation Army

*

10. What Year Was It? _____

Cigarette commercials banned from TV

The movies: *Patton* and *The French Connection*

Charles Manson found guilty in the Sharon Tate murder

Prison uprising in Attica prison

Answers
1. 1979 2. 1977 3. 1975 4. 1973 5. 1970
6. 1976 7. 1972 8. 1978 9. 1974 10. 1971

32
Growing Older

Old age is an island surrounded by death.
Juan Montalvo

*

Some old men, by continually praising the time of their youth, would almost persuade us that there were no fools in those days; but unluckily, they are left themselves for examples.

*

Aging seems to be the only available way to live a long time.
Daniel-François-Esprit Auber

*

Old age is the most unexpected of all the things that happen to a man.
Trotsky

*

Old men think themselves cunning.
Thomas Fuller

*

In the morning, we carry the world like Atlas; at noon, we stoop and bend beneath it; and at night, it crushes us flat to the ground.

Henry Ward Beecher

*

One should never count the years—one should instead count one's interests. I have kept young trying never to lose my childhood sense of wonderment. I am glad I still have a vivid curiosity about the world I live in.

Helen Keller

*

Being young is beautiful, but being old is comfortable.

Ebner-Eschenbach

*

When I was young I pitied the old. Now old, it is the young I pity.

Jean Rostand

*

Measure life by its breadth, not by its length.

*

I never heard of an old man forgetting where he buried his money.

Cicero

*

If wrinkles must be written upon our brows, let them not be written upon the heart. The spirit should not grow old.

James A. Garfield

*

We grow too soon old and too late smart.

*

Nobody loves life like an old man.

Sophocles

*

In youth the days are short and the years are long; in old age the years are short and the days are long.

Panin

*

To know how to grow old is the master work of wisdom, and one of the most difficult chapters in the great art of living.

Henri Frederick Amiel

*

My only fear is that I may live too long.

Thomas Jefferson

*

It's no secret—the people who live long are those who long to live.

*

What's important is not the years in your life but the life in your years.

*

Man arrives as a novice at each age of his life.

Nicholas Chamfort

*

Life was a funny thing that occurred on the way to the grave.

Quentin Crisp

*

A long illness seems to be placed between life and death, in order to make death a comfort both to those who die and to those who remain.

Jean de La Bruyere

*

Body and mind, like man and wife, do not always agree to die together.

Charles C. Colton

*

In age we talk much because we have seen much, and soon after shall cease talking forever.

Joseph Hall

*

The riddle of the age has for each a private solution.

Emerson

*

A little work, a little sweating, a few brief, flying years; a little joy, a little fretting, some smiles and then some tears; a little resting in the shadow, a struggle to the height, a futile search for El Dorado, and then we say Good Night.

Walt Mason

*

As many a too industrious millionaire has discovered, one cannot learn to idle at the age of 50.

Robert Lynd

33

The Last Word

All ye who stop to read this stone
Consider how soon she was gone.
Death doth not always warning give
Therefore be careful how you live.

Mary Richards

*

Die, my dear doctor! That's the last thing
I shall do!

Lord Palmerston

*

Where is the heart that doth not keep,
Within its inmost core,
Some fond remembrance hidden deep,
Of days that are no more!

Ellen Clementine Howarth

*

We are but tenants, and…shortly the great
Landlord will give us notice that our lease has
expired.

Joseph Jefferson

*

Sacred to the memory of Henry Harris, who died from a kick by a colt in his bowels. Peaceable and quiet, a friend to his father and mother, respected by all who knew him—gone to the world where horses don't kick, where sorrow and weeping are no more.

*

None could hold a candle to him.

John Edwards

*

Here lies a most beautiful lady,
Light of step and heart was she;
I think she was the most beautiful lady
That ever was in the West Country.

Walter De La Mare

*

If tombstones told the truth, everybody would wish to be buried at sea.

*

John Newton, clerk, once an infidel and Libertine, a servant of slaves in Africa,
Was by the rich mercy of our Lord and Savior Jesus Christ

Preserved, restored, pardoned, and appointed to Preach the faith he had long labored to destroy.

∗

Time was I stood where thou dost now,
And viewed the dead, as thou dost me;
Ere long thou'lt be as low as I,
And others stand and look on thee.

∗

He is not here
But only his pod:
He shelled out his peas
And went to his God.

∗

Life is a jest, and all things show it;
I thought so once, and now I know it.

∗

The words on the grave of a guide who died while climbing the Alps were "He died climbing."

∗

On the tomb of a Christian astronomer were these words (by his partner): "We have gazed too long at the stars together to be afraid of the night."

✳

While on earth my knee was lame,
I had to nurse and heed it.
But now I'm at a better place,
Where I don't even need it.

✳

Go home, dear friends
Wipe off your tears
Here I must lie
Till Christ appears.

✳

Our Little Charlie
He dropped into our world
To taste life's bitter cup,
But turned his little head aside
Disgusted with the taste and died.

✳

Poorly lived,
And poorly died,
Poorly buried,
And no one cried.

*

Stranger, as you pass o'er this grass;
Think seriously, with no humdrumming,
Prepare for death, for judgment's coming.

*

Here lies removed from mundane scenes,
A major of the King's Marines,
Under arrest in narrow borders,
He rises not till further orders.

*

I have lodged in many a town
And traveled many a year,
Till age and death have brought me down
To my last lodging here.

Joseph Horton, peddler

*

Here lies the body of Jonathan Ground,
Who was lost at sea and never found.

*

A man once lived the kind of life that
inspired his friends to place this epitaph at his
grave:
Unawed by opinion,
Unseduced by flattery,
Undismayed by disaster,
He confronted life with courage,
And death with Christian hope.

*

On a bishop's gravestone:
Here rests a man who never rested here.

*

Here a mound suffices for one for whom
the world was not large enough.

Alexander the Great

*

So little done, so much to do.

Cecil Rhodes

*

Here lies Irvin S. Cobb, not that it makes
any difference.

Irvin S. Cobb

*

Elizabeth Scott lies buried here.
She was born November 20, 1785,
according to the best of her
recollection.

*

Like a worn-out type, he is returned to the
Founder in the hope of being recast in a
better and more perfect mold.

*

God took our flower,
Our little Nell;
He thought He too
Would like a smell.

*

A man with God is always in the majority.

John Knox

*

Reading the epitaphs, our only salvation lies in resurrecting the dead and burying the living.

Paul Eldridge

*

Is this dying? Is this all? Is this all that I feared, when I prayed against a hard death? Oh, I can bear this! I can bear it! I can bear it!

Cotton Mather

*

Teach me to live, that I may dread
The grave as little as my bed.

Thomas Ken

*

Here lies
Captain Ernest Bloomfield
Accidentally shot by his Orderly
March 2, 1789
"Well done, thou good and faithful ser-
vant."

*

On a two-week-old baby's gravestone:
Came in,
Looked about;
Didn't like it
Went out.

Suffolk

*

Passerby,
Stop and think,
I'm in eternity,
You're on
the brink.

34

The Fountain of Youth

When you feel like criticizing the younger generation, just remember who raised them.

*

There is nothing wrong with the young folks that the old folks haven't outgrown.

*

We expect modern youth to be strong, courageous, and prepared to pay even more taxes than their fathers.

*

The best substitute for experience is being 17 years old.

*

It seldom occurs to teenagers that someday they will know as little as their parents.

✳

In America the young are always ready to give to those who are older than themselves the full benefits of their inexperience.

✳

He who in youth is idle will experience hardships in old age.

✳

Grown-ups can no longer tell secrets in front of you by spelling words.

✳

When we're young we want to change the world. When we're old we want to change the young.

✳

There's nothing wrong with teenagers that reasoning with them won't aggravate.

✳

Parents of teens soon discover that youth is stranger than fiction.

✳

If youth is a fault one soon gets rid of it.
Goethe

*

The old believe everything; the middle-aged suspect everything; the young know everything.

Oscar Wilde

*

The young always have the same problem—how to rebel and conform at the same time. They have solved this by defying their parents and copying one another.

Quentin Crisp

*

Youth is a malady of which one becomes cured a little every day.

Benito Mussolini

*

The question we do not see when we are young is whether we own pride or are owned by it.

Josephine Johnson

*

We are only young once. That is all society can stand.

Bob Bowen

✳

What you long for in youth, you get aplenty in old age.

Goethe

✳

It is absurd to talk of the ignorance of youth. The only people to whose opinions I listen now with any respect are people much younger than myself. They seem in front of me.

Oscar Wilde

✳

Youth is a disease that must be borne with patience! Time, indeed, will cure it.

R. H. Benson

✳

I never felt that there was anything enviable in youth. I cannot recall that any of us, as youths, admired our condition to excess or had a desire to prolong it.

Bernard Berenson

✳

A generation without a cause in its youth has no legacy in its old age.

Edward M. Kennedy

*

Even the youngest of us may be wrong
sometimes.

Bernard Shaw

*

I remember my youth and the feeling that
will never come back anymore—the feeling
that I could last forever, outlast the sea, the
earth, and all men.

Joseph Conrad

*

There is nothing wrong with the younger
generation that becoming a taxpayer won't
cure.

Dan Bennett

*

It's all that the young can do for the old,
to shock them and keep them up to date.

G. B. Shaw

*

Youth would be an ideal state if it came a
little later in life.

*

The young men of this land are often called a "lost" race—they are a race that has never yet been discovered. And the whole secret, power, and knowledge of their own discovery is locked within them—they know it, feel it, have the whole thing in them—and they cannot utter it.

Thomas Wolfe

*

The hardest job kids face today is learning good manners without seeing any.

Fred Astaire

*

Nothing so dates a man as to decry the younger generation.

Adlai Stevenson

*

You're only young once, but you can always be immature.

Dave Barry

*

To get back one's youth, one has merely to repeat one's follies.

Oscar Wilde

*

Youth is the time for the adventures of the body, but age for the triumphs of the mind.
Logan Pearsall Smith

*

Youth lasts much longer than young people think.
Diane Comtesse

35

More Old-Timers

There is many a good tune played on an old fiddle.

*

One way to reach old age is to quit feeling responsible for the entire world.

*

One of the paradoxes of life is that the young are always wishing they were just a little older and the old are usually wishing they were a whole lot younger.

*

Old age: When your memory is short, your experience long, your breath short, your eyesight dim, and your safe-deposit box full.

*

The best way to tell a woman's age is in a low whisper.

❋

Old age has one consolation: It doesn't last forever.

❋

"Old age is coming on me rapidly," the urchin said when he was stealing an apple from an old man's garden, and saw the owner coming.

❋

Old-timer: A person who can remember when people rested on Sunday instead of Monday.

❋

Aging is when you've come a long way, baby, and you just ran out of gas.

❋

Grow old along with me!
The best is yet to be,
The last of life, for which the first was made.
                          Robert Browning

❋

The fountain of youth is full as paint.
Methuselah is my favorite saint.
I've never been so comfortable before.
Oh I'm so glad I'm not young anymore.
                          Alan Jay Lerner

*

In the central place of every heart there is a recording chamber; so long as it receives messages of beauty, hope, cheer, and courage, so long are you young. When the wires are all down and your heart is covered with the snows of pessimism and the ice of cynicism, then, and then only, are you grown old.

General Douglas MacArthur

*

Old people shouldn't eat health foods. They need all the preservatives they can get.

Robert Orben

*

Don't complain about growing old—many people don't have that privilege.

Earl Warren

*

When I no longer thrill to the first snow of the season, I'll know I'm growing old.

Lady Bird Johnson

*

How foolish to think that one can ever slam the door in the face of age. Much wiser to be polite and gracious and ask him to lunch in advance.

Noel Coward

✳

Growing older is not upsetting; being perceived as old is.

Kenny Rogers

✳

Every old man complains of the growing depravity of the world, of the petulance and insolence of the rising generation.

Dr. Johnson

✳

An old man looks permanent, as if he had been born an old man.

H. E. Bates

✳

No skill or art is needed to grow old; the trick is to endure it.

Goethe

✳

My diseases are an asthma and a dropsy and, what is less curable, 75.

Samuel Johnson

✳

At 40 I lost my illusions,
At 50 I lost my hair,

At 60 my hope and teeth were gone,
And my feet were beyond repair.
At 80 life has clipped my claws,
I'm bent and bowed and cracked;
but I can't give up the ghost because
My follies are intact.

E. Y. Harburg

*

I can live with my arthritis, and my dentures fit me fine. I can see with my bifocals, but
I sure do miss my mind.

*

I'm Fine
There is nothing whatever
the matter with me.
I'm just as healthy as
I can be.
I have arthritis in back
and knees
And when I talk, I talk
with a wheeze.
My pulse is weak, my
blood is thin.
But I'm awfully well
for the shape I'm in.
My teeth eventually
had to come out,
And my diet I hate
to think about.

I'm overweight and I
can't get thin.
My appetite is sure to win.
But I'm awfully well
for the shape I'm in.

*

Since more than half my hopes came true
And more than half my fears
Are but the pleasant laughing-stock
Of these my middle years:
Shall I not bless the middle years?
Not I for youth repine
While warmly round me cluster lives
More dear to me than mine.

Sarah N. Cleghorn

36

Middle-Age Crazies

Middle age is actually the prime of life. It just takes a little longer to get primed.

＊

The terrible thing about middle age is that you'll outgrow it!

＊

Middle age is when you don't need a roomful of antiques to sit down on something 50 years old!

＊

Middle age: When your tripping becomes less light and more fantastic.

＊

Middle age is the time when the thing you grow most in your garden is tired.

＊

Childhood: That time of life when you make funny faces in the mirror.

Middle age: That time of life when the mirror gets even.

*

Middle age is that time of life when you can afford to lose a golf ball, but you can't hit it that far.

*

You have reached middle age when you try to find out where the action is so you can go somewhere else.

*

Forget about jets, racing cars, and speed-boats. Nothing goes as fast as middle age.

*

Middle age is when you begin to wonder who put the quicksand into the hourglass of time.

*

Middle age is that terrible feeling that comes over you when you're talking to your son and he says, "What's a running board?"

*

Middle age is when work is a lot less fun and fun is a lot more work!

*

Middle age is when a man has enough financial security to wear the flashy sports coats he didn't have the courage to wear when he was young.

37

Memory Madness

I have a photographic memory....It's just that I'm out of film.

*

Memory: The thing you have to forget with.

*

The older a man gets, the farther he had to walk to school as a boy.

*

"The horror of that moment," the King went on, "I shall never, never forget!" "You will, though," the Queen said, "if you don't make a memorandum of it."

Lewis Carroll

*

A retentive memory may be good thing, but the ability to forget is the true token of greatness.

Elbert Hubbard

*

Lending money to friends causes them to lose their memories.

Laurence J. Peter

*

I believe the true function of age is memory. I'm recording as fast as I can.

Rita Mae Brown

*

A strong memory is commonly coupled with infirm judgment.

Montaigne

*

Everybody needs his memories. They keep the wolf of insignificance from the door.

Saul Bellow

*

I've a grand memory for forgetting.

Robert Louis Stevenson

*

Nothing is more common than a fool with a strong memory.

C. C. Colton

*

There is a wicked inclination in most people to suppose an old man decayed in his intellect. If a young or middle aged man, when leaving a company, does not recollect where he laid his hat, it is nothing; but if the same inattention is discovered in an old man, people will shrug up their shoulders, and say, "His memory is going."

Samuel Johnson

*

There are lots of people who mistake their imagination for their memory.

Josh Billings

*

Everyone complains of his memory, but no one complains of his judgment.

La Rochefoucauld

*

Memory performs the impossible for man; holds together past and present, gives continuity and dignity to human life. This is the companion, this the tutor, the poet, the library, with which you travel.

Mark Van Doren

*

Nothing is more responsible for the good old days than a bad memory.

Robert Benchley

*

The older you get, the greater you were.

Lee Grosscup

*

There are times when forgetting can be just as important as remembering—and even more difficult.

Harry and Joan Mier

*

One form of loneliness is to have a memory and no one to share it with.

Phyllis Rose

*

Memory is the diary we all carry about with us.

Oscar Wilde

*

God gave us our memories so that we might have roses in December.

James M. Barrie

*

H: We met at nine.

G: We met at eight.

H: I was on time.

G: No, you were late.

H: Ah yes! I remember it well.

Alan Jay Lerner

*

A lot of people mistake a short memory for a clear conscience.

Doug Larson

*

He who believes that the past cannot be changed has not yet written his memories.

Torvald Gahlin

*

How is it that our memory is good enough to retain the least triviality that happens to us, and yet not good enough to recollect how often we have told it to the same person.

La Rochefoucauld

38

Name the Year Quiz—
The 1980s

1.   What Year Was It? _____

The Phantom of the Opera debuts

Les Miserables wins eight awards

Prince Andrew and Sarah Ferguson marry

The Oprah Winfrey Show becomes the highest-rated TV talk show

*

2.   What Year Was It? _____

The movie: *The Empire Strikes Back*

Pac-Man video game becomes a big hit

Dallas becomes the top-rated show

Kramer vs. Kramer wins an Academy Award

John Lennon is killed

Sinatra captures the country with "New York, New York"

*

3. What Year Was It? _____

Lionel Richie and Michael Jackson write "We Are the World"

Bill Gates becomes the world's richest billionaire

Nintendo is introduced

The movie: *Out of Africa*

Vigilante Bernhard Goetz is charged only with illegal gun possession

*

4. What Year Was It? _____

Trio album features Dolly Parton, Emmylou Harris, and Linda Ronstadt

The movie: *The Color Purple*

The movie: *The Last Emperor*

The movie: *Full Metal Jacket*

*

5.   What Year Was It? _____

U.S. Surgeon General C. Everett Koop denounces smoking

Braniff Airlines goes bankrupt

The movie: *E.T.*

The Vietnam War Memorial is dedicated in Washington, DC

*

6.   What Year Was It? _____

Prozac is first marketed

Andy Warhol's art collection sells for 25 million dollars

TV evangelist Jimmy Swaggart admits visiting a prostitute

The song "Don't Worry, Be Happy" gets a Grammy

Grunge music is developed

*

7.   What Year Was It? _____

Digital sound is introduced

The cell-phone revolution begins

M*A*S*H ends after 251 episodes

Ecstasy replaces LSD as a psychedelic drug

*

8.   What Year Was It? _____

Broadway: *Miss Saigon*

The movie: *Batman*

The movie: *Dead Poets Society*

The movie: *Driving Miss Daisy*

*

9.   What Year Was It? _____

Cabbage Patch dolls debut

The movie: *Indiana Jones and the Temple of Doom*

Reeboks, the Madonna look, Ray-Ban sunglasses, and the yuppie look catch on

Michael Jackson wins Grammy for *Thriller*

*

10. What Year Was It? _____

John Hinckley shoots President Reagan

Cats debuts on Broadway

The movie: *Raiders of the Lost Ark*

Prince Charles and Princess Diana announce their engagement

IBM introduces the first personal computer

*

Answers
1. 1986 2. 1980 3. 1985 4. 1987 5. 1982
6. 1988 7. 1983 8. 1989 9. 1984 10. 1981

39

The Making of a Life

Dost thou love life? Then do not squander time, for that's the stuff life is made of.

Benjamin Franklin

*

Life is either a daring adventure, or nothing....Security is mostly a superstition. It does not exist in nature.

Helen Keller

*

A life spent making mistakes is not only more honorable but more useful than a life spent doing nothing.

George Bernard Shaw

*

Only a life lived for others is a life worthwhile.

Albert Einstein

*

We make a living by what we get, but we make a life by what we give.

Norman MacEwan

*

One of the secrets of a happy life is continuous small treats.

Iris Murdoch

*

Life is short and we never have enough time for gladdening the hearts of those who travel the way with us. Oh, be swift to love! Make haste to be kind.

Henri Frederic Amiel

*

I am convinced that life is 10 percent what happens to me and 90 percent how I react to it.

Charles Swindoll

*

During the first period of a man's life the greatest danger is: *not to take the risk.*

Kierkegaard

*

We act as though comfort and luxury were the chief requirements of life, when all that we need to make us really happy is something to be enthusiastic about.

Charles Kingsley

*

Life is a series of surprises, and would not be worth taking or keeping if it were not.

Emerson

*

Life is made up of sobs, sniffles, and smiles, with sniffles predominating.

O. Henry

*

One of the secrets of a long and fruitful life is to forgive everybody everything every night before you go to bed.

Ann Landers

*

He is the happiest man who can trace an unbroken connection between the end of his life and the beginning.

Goethe

*

The happiness of your life depends upon the quality of your thoughts.

Marcus Antonius

*

Do not take life too seriously. You will never get out of it alive.

Elbert Hubbard

*

The hardest thing to learn in life is which bridge to cross and which to burn.

Laurence J. Peter

*

When people are serving, life is no longer meaningless.

John Gardner

*

The grand essentials to happiness in this life are something to do, something to love, and something to hope for.

Joseph Addison

*

There are only two ways to live your life. One is as though nothing is a miracle. The other is as though everything is a miracle.

Albert Einstein

*

Life can only be understood backwards; but it must be lived forwards.

Kierkegaard

*

The secret of life is to have a task, something you devote your entire life to, something you bring everything to, every minute of the day for the rest of your life. And the most important thing is, it must be something you cannot possibly do.

Henry Moore

*

The most important things in life aren't things.

*

The value of life lies not in the length of days, but in the use we make of them; a man may live long yet live very little.

Montaigne

40

You Know You're Past Middle Age When...

You know you're past middle age when... you weigh exactly the same amount as you did in high school—until you put your other foot on the scale.

*

You know you're past middle age when... you can't see the numbers on the bathroom scale without sucking in your stomach.

*

You know you're past middle age when... all of your children have moved out—and back again.

*

You know you're past middle age when... you spend a lot of time dealing with nose hair.

*

You know you're past middle age when... you start jogging with ID.

*

You know you're past middle age when...
you consider nine holes of miniature golf rigorous exercise.

*

You know you're past middle age when...
all you talk about is your cholesterol count.

*

You know you're past middle age when...
raising your arms counts as exercise.

*

You know you're past middle age when...
you start considering hair implants.

*

You know you're past middle age when...
your wife sees no difference when you suck in your stomach.

*

You know you're past middle age when...
you take vitamins regularly.

*

You know you're past middle age when...
you can tell your friends the same joke over
and over and over.

*

You know you're past middle age when...
you throw away your fake ID.

*

You know you're past middle age when...
you have no more embarrassing birds-and-
bees discussions with your kids.

*

You know you're past middle age when...
you wander the mall parking lot, searching for
your car.

*

You know you're past middle age when...
you can't be drafted and you can't even enlist.

*

You know you're past middle age when...
you no longer care that you didn't have a date
for the senior prom.

*

You know you're past middle age when...
it can take up to 15 minutes to climb out of a
hammock.

*

You know you're past middle age when...
you decide procrastination is the best approach to life, but you never get around to it.

*

You know you're past middle age when...
everything about you is starting to click: your
knees, your elbows, your neck...

*

You know you're past middle age when...
you know the difference between HDL and
LDL.

*

You know you're past middle age when...
your knees pop when you walk.

*

You know you're past middle age when...
you love going to all-you-can-eat buffet restaurants with dessert bars.

*

You know you're past middle age when...
you and your spouse resolve the "empty nest"
syndrome by becoming lovebirds.

*

You know you're past middle age when...
you try to outdo your friends' backache sto-
ries.

41

Grins

Life would be infinitely happier if we could only be born at the age of 80 and gradually approach 18.

Mark Twain

*

As people grow older, they generally become more quiet. But of course, they have more to keep quiet about.

*

Swim, dance a little, go to Paris every August, and live within walking distance of two hospitals.

Horatio Luro

*

On our fortieth wedding anniversary my wife said warmly and affectionately, "Will you love me when I'm old and gray?"

"Well, of course," I assured her. "Haven't I loved you through four other colors?"

*

Trim figures: What some people do when they tell their age.

*

Today isn't the first day of the rest of your life. It's Tuesday.

*

How old would you be if you didn't know how old you was?

*

If you want to know how old a woman is... ask her sister-in-law.

Edgar Howe

*

Life begins at 40—but so do fallen arches, lumbago, faulty eyesight, and the tendency to tell a story to the same person three or four times.

Bill Feather

*

One should never trust a woman who tells her real age. A woman who would tell one that, would tell one anything.

Oscar Wilde

*

You know how you can tell whether a woman's had her face lifted? Every time she crosses her legs, her mouth snaps open.

Joan Rivers

*

I am a hundred and two years of age. I have no worries since my youngest son went into an old folks' home.

Victoria Bedwell

*

I am 46, and have been for some time past.

Anita Brookner

*

I hope I look as good as my mother does when I reach the age she says she isn't.

*

"You're an old man!" "I'm old? When you were young, the Dead Sea was only sick!"

*

When she told me her age I believed her— why not? She hasn't changed her story for five years.

*

The older you get, the greater you were.

Lee Grosscup

*

I'm at that age where if you flattened out all the wrinkles, I'd be seven feet tall.

Robert Orben

*

When you're young and you fall off a horse you may break something. When you're my age and you fall, you splatter.

Roy Rogers

*

To get back my youth I would do anything in the world, except take exercise, get up early, or be respectable.

*

I'm not sure I'm getting wrinkles. It's possible that my skin is turning to corduroy!

*

Things ain't what they used to be and probably never was.

Will Rogers

*

Why is it that we rejoice at a birth and grieve at a funeral? It is because we are not the person involved.

Mark Twain

*

First thing I do when I wake up in the morning is breathe on a mirror and hope it fogs.

Earl Wynn

*

When people tell you how young you look, they are also telling you how old you are.

Cary Grant

*

What a relief! For the last three months I've been saving up my breath to blow out those candles.

*

After quite a bout, my doctor said, "You've been a very sick man. In fact, it was your strong constitution that pulled you through."

"That's good to know," I replied. "I trust you will keep that in mind when you make out my bill."

✳

A police officer pulled 86-year-old Mrs. West over to the curb. "You weren't using your turn-signal lights," he said politely. "First you put your hand out as if you were going to turn left, then you waved your hand up and down, and then you turned right."

Mrs. West explained, "I decided not to turn left, and when my hand was going up and down, I was erasing the left turn."

✳

Terry and Gary were annoyed by an unusually elderly twosome in front of them on the golf course. One of the pair diddled and dawdled on the fairway, while the other was searching diligently through the rough.

"Hey," shouted Terry impatiently, "why don't you help your friend find his ball?"

"He's got his ball," replied the old man. "He's looking for his club."

✳

Times have changed. Forty years ago we worked 12 hours a day and it was called economic slavery. Today, we work 14 hours a day and it's called moonlighting.

*

A five-year-old girl, returning home from a funeral of her grandmother, rode in a car with her other grandmother. "Where did Grandma go?" she asked. "We believe she went to be with God," the other grandmother replied. "How old was she?" "She was 80 years old." "How old are you?" "I am 83." The little girl thought a bit, then said, "I hope God hasn't forgotten you!"

*

Father: Get up, son. When Lincoln was your age, do you know what he was doing?

Son: No, Dad, I don't. But I do know what he was doing when he was your age.

42

To Your Good Health

After a certain age, if you don't wake up aching in every joint, you are probably dead.

Tommy Mein

*

For someone up in years, weight lifting consists of standing up!

*

After 30, a body has a mind of its own.

Bette Midler

*

When I was 40, my doctor advised me that a man in his forties shouldn't play tennis. I heeded his advice carefully and could hardly wait until I reached 50 to start again.

Hugo Black

*

But he really tries very hard to keep in shape. He does 50 push-ups a day—not intentionally...he just falls down a lot!

*

I'm pushing 60. That's enough exercise for me.

43
Older Thoughts

Those who in their youth did not live in self-harmony, and who did not gain the true treasures of life, are later like long-legged old herons standing sadly by a lake without fish.

*

Alas! it is not the child, but the boy that generally survives in the man.

Sir Arthur Helps

*

It is so comic to hear oneself called old, even at 90 I suppose!

Alice James

*

When we are sighing for the loss of our past youth, which will return no more, let us reflect that decrepitude will come, when we shall regret the mature age we have reached and do not sufficiently value.

La Bruyere

*

Age will not be defied.

Francis Bacon

*

'Tis a maxim with me to be young as long as one can: there is nothing can pay one for that invaluable ignorance which is the companion of youth; those sanguine groundless hopes, and that lively vanity, which make all the happiness of life. To my extreme mortification I grow wiser every day.

Lady Mary Wortley Montagu

*

You are as young as your faith, as old as your doubt; as young as your self-confidence, as old as your fear; as young as your hope, as old as your despair.

*

If you're not doing something with your life, it doesn't matter how long it is.

44

Name the Year Quiz— The 1990s to 2000

1. What Year Was It? _____

Whitney Houston, Mariah Carey, and the Judds have huge hits

O. J. Simpson is tried for the murder of his wife

Jacqueline Kennedy Onassis dies

Forrest Gump wins Best Picture

*

2. What Year Was It? _____

President Bush tells the world that he doesn't like broccoli

McDonalds opens 20 outlets in Moscow

England experiences mysterious "crop circles" in its cornfields

Rap music hits the market

The movie: *Dances with Wolves*

*

3.   What Year Was It? _____

Harry Potter becomes a bestseller

Credit-card holders owe 500 billion dollars on their cards

The movie: *Mission Impossible II*

The movie: *Chicken Run*

*

4.   What Year Was It? _____

John Grisham writes *The Partner*

Princess Diana dies and sparks worldwide public mourning

Mother Theresa dies at 87

Titanic wins Best Picture

The movie: *Good Will Hunting*

＊

5.   What Year Was It? _____

Natalie Cole's album *Unforgettable* wins a Grammy

Teenage Mutant Ninja Turtles and Beanie Babies catch on

The movie: *Silence of the Lambs*

The movie: *City Slickers*

＊

6.   What Year Was It? _____

Bill Clinton plays the saxophone on the Arsenio Hall show

Serial killer Jeffrey Dahmer is sentenced to 15 consecutive life prison terms

The world population hits 5.2 billion

The Prince and Princess of Wales separate

＊

7.   What Year Was It? _____

The Citadel graduates the first woman

John Kennedy, Jr. killed in plane crash

World population reaches six billion

One billion cups of Coca-Cola served per day

*

8.   What Year Was It? _____

The movie: *The Rainmaker*

Snowboarding and in-line skating catch on

Swing dancing, the grunge look, baseball caps, backpacks, and "hip-hop" catch on

The book: *Men Are from Mars, Women Are from Venus*

*

9.   What Year Was It? _____

Whitney Houston: "I Will Always Love You"

Ruth Bader Ginsburg appointed to U.S. Supreme Court

The movie: *A Few Good Men*

The movie: *Aladdin*

Schindler's List wins Best Picture

*

10. What Year Was It? _____

Eric Clapton: *Change the World*

John Grisham: *The Runaway Jury*

Prince Charles and Princess Diana agree to divorce

Nike Air Jordans become a fad

The movie: *The English Patient*

*

11. What Year Was It? _____

The FDA approves Viagra

Frank Sinatra dies

Americans each average 2300 phone calls a year

E.R, Friends, 60 Minutes, and *NYPD Blue* become hit TV programs

Answers
1. 1994 2. 1990 3. 2000 4. 1997 5. 1991
6. 1992 7. 1999 8. 1995 9. 1993 10. 1996
11. 1998

45

The Last Laugh

Shall wee all die?
Wee shall die all.
All die shall we?
Die all we shall.

*

Here lies Groucho Marx
and Lies and Lies and Lies.
P.S. He never kissed an ugly girl.

*

Erected to the memory of John MacFarlane
Drowned in the Water of Leith
By a few affectionate friends.

*

Even a tombstone will say good things
about a fellow when he is down.

*

Blown upward
Out of sight
He sought the leak
by Candlelight

*

He was young
He was fair
But the Injuns
Raised his hair.

*

Hanged by mistake.

George Johnson

*

On the gravestone of a gardener:
Transplanted

*

FEAR GOD
Keep the commandments, and
Don't attempt to climb a tree,
For that's what caused the death of me.

*

Here lies Matthew Mudd,
Death did him no hurt;
When alive he was Mudd
And now he's dead he's but dirt.

*

John Carnegie lies here,
Descended from Adam and Eve;

If any can boast of a pedigree higher,
He will willingly give them leave.

*

This man died at 30; he was buried at 70.

*

He died trying
She died wanting things

And on the grave next to hers:
He died trying to give them to her.

*

Here lie the remains of JOHN HALL,
Grocer,
The world is not worth a fig, and
I have good raisins for saying so.

*

On the gravestone of a coal miner:
Gone underground for good.

*

At rest beneath this slab of stone
lies stingy James A. Wyett.
He died one morning just at ten
And saved a dinner by it.

*

Pull out a gray hair and seven will come to its funeral.

*

My life's been hard
And all things show it;
I always thought so
And now I know it.

*

Here lies the mother of children seven,
Four on earth and three in heaven;
The three in heaven preferring rather
To die with mother than live with father.

46

Time to Retire

An old football coach, who had always been very energetic and successful, finally retired. When someone asked him, "Coach, how do you like it?" he replied, "It's great! Now I don't do anything—and I don't start till noon."

*

Retirement is the time of life when you can stop lying about your age and start lying about the house.

*

Q: What's the worst part of doing nothing?
A: You can't take the day off.

*

We could all retire comfortably if we could sell our experience for what it cost us.

*

Retirement security: Making sure all the doors are locked before you go to bed.

*

Sixty-five—that's the age when you've acquired enough experience to lose your job.

*

Work is the recreation of the retired.

*

It is by no accident that, when someone meets someone for the first time, "How do you do?" is usually closely followed by "What do you do?" Since most working people describe themselves by the company or organization to which they belong, work makes them "somebody"; unemployed people become "nobodies."

The importance of this job-related identification shows up when a person retires. Scientists attribute much of the trauma associated with retirement to a sudden loss of identity.

*

Retirement, we understand, is great if you are busy, rich, and healthy. But then, under those conditions, work is great too.

Bill Vaughan

*

Few men of action have been able to make
a graceful exit at the appropriate time.

Malcolm Muggeridge

*

Retirement should be based on the tread,
not the mileage.

Allen Ludden

*

There is nothing worse than being a doer
with nothing to do.

Elizabeth Layton

*

Retirement at 65 is ridiculous! When I was
65, I still had pimples!

George Burns

*

If you want a carefree life, retire—and
forget to tell your wife.

Eugene P. Bertin

*

Retired s being tired twice, I've thought,
First tired of working,
Then tired of not

Richard Armour

*

Retirement must be wonderful. I mean, you can suck in your stomach for only so long.

Burt Reynolds

*

When a man retires and time is no longer a matter of urgent importance, his colleagues generally present him with a watch.

R. C. Sherriff

*

Don't simply retire from something; have something to retire to.

Harry Emerson Fosdick

*

With retirement, one should have on hand two or three jobs that ought to be done, and that he wants to get done, but which do not have to be done today. Once these are provided, he can experience the true joys of procrastination.

Wheeler McMillen

*

A retired husband is often a wife's full-time job.

Ella Harriss

47

Last Thoughts

You know you're getting older when you get tired brushing your teeth.

*

You know you're getting older when reminiscing becomes the art of combining fact with fiction and it produces fantasy.

*

You know you're getting older when your favorite music is only available on 33 rpm vinyl records.

*

You know you're getting older when archaeologists dig up things you remember from your childhood.

*

You know you're getting older when your birth certificate is written in Roman numerals.

*

You know you're getting older when you begin to sleep between your naps.

*

You know you're getting older when you begin to enter your fourth childhood.

*

You know you're getting older when strangers begin to call you Granddad or Grandma.

*

You know you're getting older when you have bunions on your bunions.

*

You know you're getting older when your grandchildren ask you if you ever had a pet dinosaur.

*

You know you're getting older when you begin to round your age down to the nearest decade.

*

You know you're getting older when you finally find what you were looking for but you have forgotten why you wanted it.

*

You know you're getting older when you approach middle age for the third time.

*

You know you're getting older when your beautician sends you a note and it says, "Dear Customer, I can no longer help you. From this day on you're on your own."

*

You know you're getting older when you enjoy hearing "You Know You're Getting Older" jokes.

*

Just a reminder...that kissing for older people should never be done unless both parties have their false teeth in.

*

One of the advantages of growing older is that you get to ride at top speed on ambulances.

*

Still another advantage of growing older is that you can get your children to do all of your shopping and housework for you by suggesting that you might move in with them. You can even suggest that your nicest relatives will be rewarded in your will.

*

One of the greatest advantages of growing older is that, by virtue of your advanced years, you have become a fountain of knowledge on positively everything.

*

The fortunate advantage of growing older is that the louder your snoring becomes your spouse's hearing deteriorates at the same rate.

*

The other day someone suggested that even my toupee was turning gray.

*

It's amazing. We have the technology to put men on the moon but cannot create a wig that can't be detected by a shortsighted person from the other side of a darkened room

*

I took a memory test the other day. It asked if I could remember the day I was born. It also asked if I could remember all the days of the week. After answering the second question, I had a vague recollection of starting the test.

*

Senescence begins
And middle age ends
The day your descendants
Outnumber your friends.

Ogden Nash

*

The new nursery rhyme goes:
Old Mother Hubbard
Went to the cupboard
To fetch her poor dog a bone
But when she got there
She forgot why she'd gone
So she made herself a nice
Ham-and-cheese-on-rye sandwich.

*

Did you hear about the newspaper reporter who wanted to do a story on growing older? He spotted a little old man rocking in a chair on his porch. "I couldn't help noticing how happy you look," he said. "May I ask you your secret for a long and happy life?"

The man replied, "I smoke three packs of cigarettes a day, I drink a case of alcohol a week, I eat fatty foods and lots of desserts. And I never do any exercise."

"That's amazing," said the reporter. "May I ask how old you are?"

"Twenty-six," he said.

Other Books by Bob Phillips

For more information, send a self-addressed stamped envelope to:

Family Services
P.O. Box 9363
Fresno, California 93702